# THE EVERYTHING® LARGE-PRINT GAMES & PUZZLES

BOOK

### 150+ Crossword, Word Search, Sudoku, and Logic Games for Unlimited Puzzle Fun!

**Charles Timmerman,** Founder of Funster.com

Adams Media

New York   London   Toronto   Sydney   New Delhi

Adams Media
An Imprint of Simon & Schuster, LLC
100 Technology Center Drive
Stoughton, Massachusetts 02072

Copyright © 2024 by Simon & Schuster, LLC.

An Everything® Series Book.

Everything® and everything.com® are registered trademarks of Simon & Schuster, LLC.

First Adams Media trade paperback edition June 2024

ADAMS MEDIA and colophon are registered trademarks of Simon & Schuster, LLC.

Simon & Schuster: Celebrating 100 Years of Publishing in 2024

For information about special discounts for bulk purchases, please contact Simon & Schuster Special Sales at 1-866-506-1949 or business@simonandschuster.com.

The Simon & Schuster Speakers Bureau can bring authors to your live event. For more information or to book an event, contact the Simon & Schuster Speakers Bureau at 1-866-248-3049 or visit our website at www.simonspeakers.com.

Interior design by Colleen Cunningham

Manufactured in the United States of America

10 9 8 7 6 5 4 3 2 1

ISBN 978-1-5072-2248-5

Contains material adapted from the following titles published by Adams Media, an Imprint of Simon & Schuster, LLC: *The Everything® 15-Minute Sudoku Book* by Charles Timmerman, copyright © 2006, ISBN 978-1-59869-054-5; *The Everything® 30-Minute Sudoku Book* by Charles Timmerman, copyright © 2006, ISBN 978-1-59869-055-2; *The Everything® Large-Print Crosswords Book, Volume III* by Charles Timmerman, copyright © 2012, ISBN 978-1-4405-3890-2; *The Everything® Large-Print Word Search Book, Volume IV* by Charles Timmerman, copyright © 2012, ISBN 978-1-4405-3885-8; *The Everything® Logic Puzzles Book, Volume 1* by Marcel Danesi, PhD, copyright © 2017, ISBN 978-1-5072-0414-6; and *The Everything® Logic Puzzles Book, Volume 2* by Marcel Danesi, PhD, copyright © 2017, ISBN 978-1-5072-0415-3.

# Contents

# Introduction

In our fast-paced world, where the constant stream of information and distractions can be overwhelming, puzzles offer an opportunity to pause, engage, and unwind. With *The Everything® Large-Print Games & Puzzles Book*, you can find a respite from the relentless buzz of modern life. Immerse yourself in the world of words, numbers, and logical deduction. Whether you're a beginner or a seasoned puzzle enthusiast, you'll find a wide range of games and challenges, including:

- **Word search** puzzles are like hidden treasure hunts. Words are hidden in a grid in any direction: up, down, forward, backward, or diagonally. Word searches are not only fun but also great for enhancing your vocabulary and memory skills. From themes like "Go Camping" to "Street Smart," each word search in this book is a unique adventure waiting to be explored.

- **Crosswords** are probably the most common word puzzles in the world. They combine the love of language with the thrill of problem-solving. Whether you like easy or challenging crosswords, you'll enjoy the satisfaction of expanding your knowledge as you revel in the fun of completing a grid.

- **Sudoku** is a number puzzle that has taken the world by storm with its simple rules and complex solutions. It's played on a 9-cell × 9-cell grid with heavier lines subdividing this grid into nine 3-cell × 3-cell boxes. The object is to fill in the grid so that every row, column, and 3-cell × 3-cell box contains the numbers one through nine with no repeats. Sudoku will test your patience, but it will also sharpen your analytical skills.

- **Logic puzzles** have been played since the dawn of history to foster logical thinking. They are enigmatic conundrums that play with pattern, arrangement, and principles of organization. They reveal what it means to deduce, infer, or conclude something from a given set of facts, but in a fun way. Each puzzle is a thrilling adventure in critical thinking, designed to stretch your cognitive abilities and foster a deeper appreciation for the beauty of logical deduction.

And in this book, everything is bigger and easier to read—the word lists, clues, numbers, grids—even the answers! So if you're tired of straining your eyes trying to read too-small type or writing in too-small grids, this oversized collection is for you! Whether you're seeking a mental workout, a moment of relaxation, or a way to improve your memory and problem-solving skills, *The Everything® Large-Print Games & Puzzles Book* is your passport to a world of mind-expanding fun. Let the games begin!

# Word Search Puzzles

ADOPTION

AQUARIUM

BIRD

BREEDER

CAGE

CARE

CATS

COLLAR

DOGS

ENJOYMENT

EXOTIC

FAMILY

FERRET

FROG

FUR

GERBIL

GOLDFISH

HAMSTER

HORSE

KITTENS

LITTER

LIZARD

LOVE

LOYAL

MEDICINE

NEUTER

OWNER

PARAKEET

PARROT

PET FOOD

PUPPY

RABBITS

REPTILES

SNAKES

SPAY

STORE

TRAINING

TURTLE

WALK

WATER

# Pet Friends

```
B M J T F Y P P U P C C P L
S E K A N S R B L H I A A O
K D L A G T E L I T T E R V
D I A D I A D H O R S E R E
P C W O F C E X T Y S G O D
E I Y P A R E T S M A H T T
T N R T M U R E P T I L E S
F E J I I F B S T O R E G N
O N G O L D F I S H K A A E
O E N N Y C O L L A R B C T
D U I W A M U I R A U Q A T
I T N B P H E A G O R F E I
X E I O S W P N C W L R F K
J R A B B I T S T N R Q Q H
D D R A Z I L U G E R B I L
E L T R U T Z B F R E T A W
```

SOLUTION PAGE 222

| | |
|---|---|
| ANIMALS | PATH |
| AXE | POLES |
| BOOTS | PONCHO |
| CABIN | RAFTING |
| CANTEEN | RAIN |
| CLOTHES | RETREAT |
| COOKING | ROPE |
| COOLER | SCOUTS |
| CRAFTS | SHELTER |
| DOME | SKITS |
| GLOVES | SNOW |
| GRILL | SOCKS |
| HAMMOCK | STAKES |
| HATCHET | STOVE |
| HIKING | SUMMER |
| INSECTS | TENT |
| LANTERN | WEATHER |
| LATRINE | WINTER |
| LOGS | WOODS |
| MATCHES | |
| NATURE | |

# Go Camping

```
H S T U O C S T N E T B N W
T J E A H L A E N X S S I E
A S U K T A S I H A O N V Q
E L N D A N R S S C T O O F
R A O I P T H T K E T U H W
T M G J A E S S R S L A R P
E I A L L R I U T O M O M E
R N G T O N E E M M P W P S
B A E F S V H H O M M E E Z
O R F E O C E C T S E H G G
O Y C T T H K S O A T R N L
T T A A I N C Q Z O E I T O
S F H X Y N A N L L K W K G
Y C L L I R G C O I J I T S
W O O D S I N O H P E D N O
R S T F A R C A B I N F F G
```

SOLUTION PAGE 222

9

| | |
|---|---|
| BELTWAY | LANE |
| BICYCLES | MAIN ROAD |
| BRAKING | MIRRORS |
| BRIDGE | PARKWAY |
| BYPATH | RACING |
| BYROAD | REST STOP |
| CAR SEAT | ROADWAY |
| CAUSEWAY | SHORTCUT |
| COASTING | SPEEDING |
| CROSSWALK | SPEEDWAY |
| CRUISING | TRAFFIC |
| CURVES | TURNOFF |
| DETOUR | TURNPIKE |
| DOWNSHIFT | YELLOW |
| DRIVEWAY | YIELD |
| FREEWAY | |
| FUEL | |
| GREEN | |
| HIGHWAY | |
| HILLS | |
| INSURANCE | |

## Street Smart

```
N V B F S R O R R I M T O F
B J Y R P E K I P N R U T F
P S P E E D I N G V L C R O
A E A E E B R I D G E T A N
R V T W D G N I S I U R C R
K R H A W P N B V A F O I U
W U T Y A O D I R E X H N T
A C R T Y T E C T A W S G N
Y W A F I S T Y A S K A K E
A O F I E T O C A R A I Y E
W L F H L S U L B W S O N R
H L I S D E R E H Y T E C G
G E C N A R U S N I R L A G
I Y A W E S U A C A L O E T
H C R O S S W A L K L L A B
Y A W D A O R N I A M D S D
```

SOLUTION PAGE 222

| | |
|---|---|
| ACTIVITY | HUM |
| APIARY | KEEPER |
| ARTIFICIAL | LARVAE |
| BEE | MUD |
| BOXES | NATURAL |
| BROOD | NEST |
| BUSY | ORDER |
| BUZZING | POLLEN |
| CELLS | PRODUCTION |
| CLAY | PROPOLIS |
| CLUSTER | PUPAE |
| COLONY | QUEEN |
| COMB | SMOKE |
| CROPS | STING |
| DRONE | STRUCTURE |
| EGGS | SWEET |
| ENCLOSED | TREE |
| FLOWERS | WAX |
| HABITAT | WORKER |
| HEXAGON | |
| HONEY | |

# Beehive

```
S Z P T R E E M I Q U E E N
B C B Y D E S O L C N E E O
E R H L W N T I W P F L A B
G O O W A O R D E R L Z M R
G P L O X I U Y N O L O C H
S S A R D T C N P P C S L W
G W R K U C T I Q O M Y A H
N E U E M U U T F L T H Y A
I E T R W D R G N I Z Z U B
T T A S I O E E V S T M X I
S A N M D R L I P X T R E T
M Y P R M P T F I E S C A A
O E O I L C L U S T E R P T
K N O G A X E H N L X K U S
E O E A V R A L L V O R P E
V H U M F I Y S U B B E E N
```

SOLUTION PAGE 222

| | |
|---|---|
| BOX | PIECES |
| CARDS | PLAY |
| CHANCE | POINTS |
| CHESS | POPULAR |
| CHILDREN | RISK |
| CLUE | ROLL |
| COUNTERS | RULES |
| DICE | SCENARIO |
| FAMILY | SCRABBLE |
| FRIENDS | SORRY |
| FUN | SPACES |
| GAME | SPIN |
| KIDS | SQUARE |
| LEARN | TABLE |
| LIFE | TIMER |
| LOSE | TOKENS |
| LUCK | TRIVIA |
| MARBLES | TURN |
| MARKER | WIN |
| MONOPOLY | |
| MOVES | |

# Games

```
U A C B T X B R U L E S D P
N I W H L I S S E V O M L L
N V Y P E N M A F U N R U T
P I E C E S R E T N U O C G
O R P K I N S Y R D P H K Y
I T O S S C E N A R I O F B
N T G X H F T A B L E S R Y
T S P A C E S O D D P E I R
S O N M M S C R A B B L E R
R C V R O E E A I S E B N O
E F I L K N N L Q C A R D S
K U R D K Q O U E I X A S U
R E L I G O A P S I O M G O
A O D C S R Q O O O B B A V
M S L E E K T P L L Q Q U L
K S M L L F A M I L Y S F T
```

SOLUTION PAGE 223

| | |
|---|---|
| BARBECUE | PICNIC |
| BENCH | PIGEONS |
| BIKERS | PLANTS |
| BLANKET | PLAYGROUND |
| CANOE | POND |
| CHILDREN | POOL |
| CLOWNS | RECREATION |
| FLOWERS | ROSES |
| GAMES | SANDBOX |
| GARDEN | SHADE |
| GAZEBO | SHELTER |
| GRASS | SKATEBOARD |
| GRILL | SLIDE |
| HOPSCOTCH | SWIMMING |
| ICE CREAM | SWINGS |
| JOGGERS | TABLES |
| JUGGLERS | |
| KITE | |
| LANDSCAPE | |
| LAWN | |
| LEMONADE | |

# A Day at the Park

```
H C N E B L A N K E T I K J
M X B D P R E T L E H S Y M
Q O I G N I M M I W S E W Q
I B K E Q O G J O G G E R S
T D E O G H P E J N P Q H P
A N R N P M O U O L A A M L
B A S A O J G P A N D D A N
L S E C O G I Y S E S W E E
E S M U L B G S P C N V R R
S V R E C R E A T I O N C D
S G R E O E C T R N C T E L
A S N U W S B R A D A N C I
R Q N I D O K R O K E L I H
G D S N W O L C A S S N P C
D G A M E S Z F O B E Z A G
L L I R G A P E D I L S C B
```

SOLUTION PAGE 223

| | |
|---|---|
| ACADEMIA | LITERATURE |
| APPLE | LOUNGE |
| ARITHMETIC | MATH |
| ASSIGNMENT | PAPER |
| ATTENDANCE | PENCIL |
| BLACKBOARD | PRINCIPAL |
| BOOK | PUPIL |
| BUS | QUIZ |
| CAMPUS | READING |
| CLASS | RECESS |
| COLLEGE | RED PEN |
| COURSE | SCHOLAR |
| CURRICULUM | STUDY |
| DESK | SUBJECT |
| EDUCATION | TEACHER |
| ENGLISH | TEST |
| EXAM | TEXT |
| GPA | VARSITY |
| GYM | WRITING |
| HOMEWORK | |
| LESSON | |

## School Time

```
T Y E X A M R M L I C N E P
E K F W I R E Y D U T S H R
A R X R M P A G S X R S V S
C O U I E A D L E U I G S U
H W M T D P I T O L P A B B
E E U I A E N C G H L M L J
R M L N C R G N A C C O A E
G O U G A L E S S O N S C C
P H C Q U I Z T S O D P K T
A C I T E M H T I R A M B E
V A R S I T Y T G L T A O G
P P R E C N A D N E T T A N
U P U T I C E G M C J H R U
P L C U U S S S E C E R D O
I E T D K P R I N C I P A L
L R E D P E N U T K O O B R
```

SOLUTION PAGE 223

| | |
|---|---|
| ANNIVERSARY | GROUP |
| APPETIZERS | GUESTS |
| BALLOONS | HALLOWEEN |
| BEER | INVITATIONS |
| BIRTHDAY | KEG |
| BLOCK PARTY | MIXER |
| CANDLES | MUSIC |
| CELEBRATION | PEOPLE |
| CHRISTMAS | RECEPTION |
| COCKTAIL | STREAMERS |
| DECORATIONS | SURPRISE |
| DRINKING | TEA PARTY |
| EATING | TEENAGERS |
| EVENT | |
| FAMILY | |
| FOOD | |
| FUN | |
| GAMES | |
| GATHERING | |
| GIFTS | |
| GRADUATION | |

## Throw a Party

```
R A P P E T I Z E R S A P R
Y G R A D U A T I O N E E G
B I R T H D A Y V N O X N F
E T N E V E R H I P I I U T
S E N Y I C B V L M T D F E
I A O L T O E E G A A R C E
R P I I G R E C E P T I O N
P A T M S A A S K R I N C A
R R A A F T T P T J V K K G
U T R F O I R H K F N I T E
S Y B Y O O Y E E C I N A R
T S E L D N A C A R O G I S
S C L C I S U M S M I L L E
E U E H A L L O W E E N B M
U T C H R I S T M A S R G A
G R O U P B A L L O O N S G
```

SOLUTION PAGE 223

| | |
|---|---|
| ACTIVE | POTENT |
| ATHLETIC | POWERFUL |
| BEEFY | ROBUST |
| BIG | RUGGED |
| BRAWNY | SECURE |
| BRUISING | SINEWY |
| BULKY | SOLID |
| CAPABLE | SOUND |
| DURABLE | STABLE |
| ENDURING | STALWART |
| ENERGETIC | STAUNCH |
| FIRM | STEADY |
| FORCEFUL | STOUT |
| FORCIBLE | STURDY |
| HEALTHY | TIRELESS |
| HEFTY | UNTIRING |
| HULKING | VIGOROUS |
| HUNK | VITAL |
| HUSKY | |
| MIGHTY | |
| MUSCULAR | |

# Powerful Words

```
B H H U S K Y S O U N D L L
E U U S E C U R E L B A T S
E N L N S E Y T N E T O P W
F K K K H E A L T H Y O V O
Y D I F Y K L B R A W N Y L
W U N O S N S E D E G G U R
E R G R U N T I R I N G G O
N A N C O R O F D I L O S B
I B I E R A U H E F T Y A U
S L R F O L T R A W L A T S
T E U U G U Y D R U T S H T
E V D L I C F O R C I B L E
A I N A V S C A P A B L E G
D T E T G U I H C N U A T S
Y C F I R M I N Y T H G I M
N A B V E N E R G E T I C D
```

SOLUTION PAGE 224

APPLE

BALLS

BRACELET

CANDY CANE

COAL

COFFEE

COLOGNE

COSMETICS

CRAYONS

DOLL

DVD

FRUIT

GAG GIFT

GAMES

GIFT CARDS

GUM

IPOD

LIPSTICK

LOTION

MONEY

NAIL POLISH

NECKLACE

NUTS

ORANGES

PENCILS

PERFUME

PUZZLE

SHAMPOO

SNOW GLOBE

SOAP

STICKERS

TEA

TOOTHBRUSH

TOYS

UNDERWEAR

WATCH

# Little Gifts

```
E J M L I P S T I C K X X P
M O N E Y L S H A M P O O K
U U X V I E E N G O L O C W
F N G C M D D L A O C Z O A
R D N A S Y O T T S F T F T
E E G M C T E L N C F A F C
P R N A I L P O L I S H E H
S W N O E U W W G T D S E C
L E N C Z G P G T E R U U W
L A A Z L A A I I M A R C Q
A R L O O G S H U S C B R P
B E B S E G N A R O T H A A
N E C K L A C E F C F T Y S
N U D O P I E A F M I O O S
M V T E P D Q T E F G O N L
D O S S A S R E K C I T S T
```

SOLUTION PAGE 224

BADGE

CAMPAIGN

CERAMIC

CLOSURE

COAT

COLLAR

COVERED

CUTE

DESIGN

DRESS

FABRIC

FASTEN

FLY

GARMENT

GLASS

HOLE

JACKET

JEANS

KNOB

LOOP

PANTS

POCKET

PUSH

ROUND

SEW

SHANK

SHIRT

SHORTS

SIZE

SKIRT

SNOWMAN

STUD

SUIT

SWEATER

# Cute As a Button

```
L C A M P A I G N C L D W E
G D E S I G N H O L E N R G
S K I R T G I A P P S U O D
G Y L F A S T E N C S O X A
U M B B H M B T P O E R Y B
Q O S A O S I G L V R U M S
K W N F H N L C A E D C J T
I K B I L A K Y Z R I U R R
K P R O S E L I A E M T B O
G T O S T J S L F D S E W H
B P L C E U L N A M W O N S
E U J Q K O H F B P E E S T
G S C P C E M W R A A H U U
P H U X A I T Q I V T N I D
Q X A K J Y U I C V E A T V
O I N K O Z Q X Q R R D U S
```

SOLUTION PAGE 224

| | |
|---|---|
| BASEBALL | MODEL CAR |
| BEACH TOYS | MONOPOLY |
| BICYCLES | MOTORCYCLES |
| BOATS | NINTENDO |
| CARD GAMES | PIANO |
| CHECKERS | PLAYSTATION |
| COLLECTIBLE | RADIO |
| COMPUTERS | SCOOTER |
| CRAFTS | SKIS |
| CRAYONS | TRAINS |
| DOLLS | VIDEO GAMES |
| EDUCATIONAL | VOLLEYBALL |
| ELECTRONICS | WATER GUNS |
| FUN | XBOX |
| GADGETS | |
| GUITAR | |
| ICE SKATES | |
| IPOD | |
| JACKS | |
| KITES | |
| LEGOS | |

# All Kinds of Toys

```
R S N U G R E T A W X B O X
A S O G E L L A B E S A B Y
T B V O L L E Y B A L L D L
I M O T O R C Y C L E S O O
U S C S R E T U P M O C L P
G K Y C O W R A D I O R L O
V B G O S D O R Z L Z A S N
C I A O T N N S L F Y Y C O
H C D T V H I E K S U O R M
E Y G E D U C A T I O N A L
C C E R O T S A R N S S F R
K L T M I G T S E T I K T S
E E S B P I A N O B H N S K
R S L H O S E M A G D R A C
S E S N D M O D E L C A R A
B O A T S E T A K S E C I J
```

SOLUTION PAGE 224

| | |
|---|---|
| ACES | KING |
| ANACONDA | KUHN |
| BET | LOW |
| BILLABONG | MIXED |
| CALL | OMAHA |
| CARD | OXFORD |
| CASINO | PAIR |
| CHIPS | PASS |
| COMMUNITY | PLAY |
| DEAL | POT |
| DECK | QUEEN |
| DEUCES | RAZZ |
| DOUBLE | ROYAL |
| DRAW | SHUFFLE |
| FIVE | SPLIT |
| FLUSH | STUD |
| GAME | TABLE |
| GUTS | TEXAS |
| HAND | WIN |
| HIGH | |
| HOLD | |

# Poker Games

```
B W Y K L B C D R O F X O M
Y I A W L D E D T H D I C Q
E N L W A U P D D L O H A A
T O P L C L A X U F A N C K
S R E E A A S Y J T A E C M
V D S P L B S T Z C S E D G
U G T A N F O I O G D U Q C
N E Y E S N F N N W N Q H J
D O M I X E D U G O S I U V
R R A Z Z A O M H L P E K Z
A H A N D C S M D S L G T X
C Y V W Y T Z O A B I D E H
V W N H U K U C A H T M B M
M I D G S B U T R I A P Q B
I A W F L U S H I G H G N V
O N W E V I F W V N W W W K
```

SOLUTION PAGE 225

| | |
|---|---|
| APOGEE | PHYSICS |
| AXIS | PLANET |
| CIRCLE | PLUTO |
| COMET | PULL |
| CURVE | RADIUS |
| CYCLE | REVOLVE |
| DEBRIS | RING |
| ELLIPSE | ROCKET |
| FOLLOW | ROTATE |
| FORCE | ROUND |
| GRAVITY | SOLAR |
| JUPITER | SPACE |
| KEPLER | SPHERE |
| MARS | STAR |
| MOON | SUN |
| MOTION | SYSTEM |
| MOVE | TRACK |
| NEPTUNE | VENUS |
| NEWTON | YEAR |
| PATH | |
| PERIOD | |

# Orbit

```
A M D S S I X A F Y M P J E
E B R P T U L K E T E M O C
S A A Q I D N U O R T O S R
M C D P Y J Z J I I S V P O
E W I F O L L O W N Y E H F
W J U M L G D T H G S H E K
V G S S L N E L C R I C R R
X D N C U R V E N U T P E N
D E S O P N S R E V O L V E
O B P C I P E Z Q Q P R T W
G R A V I T Y V C E T A R T
Y I P L I S O E K Y T T O O
H S L P Y O Y M A O C S C N
L E U P G L V H R R K L K D
G J T K C A R T P L A N E T
Z N O O M R M X K C P A T H
```

SOLUTION PAGE 225

| | |
|---|---|
| AGRICULTURE | LIVESTOCK |
| BAKED GOODS | MUSIC |
| BALLOONS | NOVELTIES |
| BLUE RIBBON | PICTURES |
| BUMPER CARS | PIZZA |
| CARNIVAL | PRIZES |
| CAROUSEL | RACES |
| CLOWNS | RIDE PASS |
| COIN TOSS | SNOW CONES |
| COMPETITIONS | SWINGS |
| CONCESSIONS | |
| CONTEST | |
| COTTON CANDY | |
| DANCERS | |
| EXHIBITS | |
| FOOD | |
| FUN | |
| GAMES | |
| HANDICRAFTS | |
| ICE CREAM | |
| LIGHTS | |

## Fun Fair

```
K S K E X H I B I T S Y B G
C O N C E S S I O N S G U A
O S S O T N I O C I S U M M
T S M S N O W C O N E S P E
S A A G R I C U L T U R E S
E P E N J T F U N H S Y R N
V E R I G I I O U A D T C O
I D C W B T V A C N O P A O
L I E S R E C N A D O I R L
I R C I L P V C R I G C S L
G W I T R M N D N C D T C A
H I I I N O B B I R E U L B
T E Z G T C H E V A K R O D
S E J T P I Z Z A F A E W O
S C O N T E S T L T B S N O
G C S E C A R O U S E L S F
```

SOLUTION PAGE 225

ARTISTS

BALLADS

BAND

BASS GUITAR

CHANTS

CHICAGO

CONCERT

COUNTRY

DRUMS

HARMONICA

HYMNS

INSTRUMENTS

JAZZ

LEAD BELLY

MAJOR SCALE

MELANCHOLY

MEMPHIS

MOOD

MUSIC GENRE

MUSICIANS

NEW ORLEANS

NOTES

PITCH

PLAY

RECORDS

ROCK

SADNESS

SAXOPHONE

SHOUTS

SINGERS

SINGING

SLOW

SPIRITUALS

TROMBONE

VOCALS

WORK SONGS

# Sing the Blues

```
P S L A U T I R I P S L O W
M L I E Y H R E C O R D S Y
E A A N A R A E S N M Y H E
M C P Y G D T R C Z Z A J N
P O C I L I B N M N G D S O
H V S W T O N E U O O U N H
I N T K O C H G L O N C A P
S E N E C R H C M L C I I O
D W E S N O K I N Y Y O C X
A O M A J O R S C A L E I A
L R U D N A B U O A L I S S
L L R N D R U M S N G E U H
A E T E N S E T O N G O M O
B A S S G U I T A R Y S D U
V N N S H A R T I S T S P T
E S I N G E R S T N A H C S
```

SOLUTION PAGE 225

| | |
|---|---|
| ACE | PETE SAMPRAS |
| ANDRE AGASSI | RAFAEL NADAL |
| ARTHUR ASHE | ROGER FEDERER |
| BOBBY RIGGS | ROLAND-GARROS |
| BORIS BECKER | SERVE |
| CLAY | SMASH |
| COURT | SPIN |
| DAVIS CUP | STEFAN EDBERG |
| DEUCE | US OPEN |
| DROP SHOT | WILD CARDS |
| FAULT | |
| GAME | |
| JIMMY CONNORS | |
| JOHN MCENROE | |
| LET | |
| LOVE | |
| MARTINA HINGIS | |
| MATCH | |
| MICHAEL CHANG | |
| NET | |
| PASSING SHOT | |

## Play Tennis

```
S T E F A N E D B E R G A L
E H S A M S W L C U N R R C
R T B U A C E U S A T S J R
V J O L R T E O H H D I E O
E B R T T D P C U R M R S L
E O I F I E L R A M E N A A
O B S K N E A C Y D E N R N
R B B Z A S D C E T D D P D
N Y E H H L O F P R L R M G
E R C E I N R U E U O O A A
C I K W N E C A E O V P S R
M G E O G S G L M C E S E R
N G R O I A I M A T C H T O
H S R V S P I N G Y T O E S
O P A S S I N G S H O T P Z
J D I R A F A E L N A D A L
```

SOLUTION PAGE 226

| ANIMATION | ORNAMENT |
|-----------|----------|
| BATTERY | OUTSIDE |
| BLINKING | PLASTIC |
| BRIGHT | PLUG |
| BULB | POWER |
| CIRCUIT | SAFETY |
| COLOR | SETS |
| COMPUTER | SHOW |
| CORD | SIGN |
| DISPLAY | SOCKET |
| ENERGY | STAR |
| FIBER | STRAND |
| FLASHING | STRING |
| FLICKER | SWITCH |
| FUSE | TIMER |
| GLASS | TREE |
| HOLIDAY | VOLTAGE |
| HOUSE | WATTS |
| LAMPS | WIRES |
| LED | |
| LIGHT | |

# Christmas Display

```
S T T A W P O W E R E B I F
S W I T C H L L S Y N Y B R
A O S T J C R U T T E G A A
L A C P R E O E G H R B I T
G N C K M E F R B O G A O S
X I S I E A E B D L Y I N T
K M T L S T L G J I U H R D
S A E X U I N T W D W B S B
G T S P N I I E I A O A E I
C I M K R U S O M Y H T R L
Q O I T C U U P L A S T I C
C N S R O T H G I L N E W O
G N I H S A L F C P G R Z L
Y C L I U N R F U S E Y O O
L E D Y N R E K C I L F L R
H E G A T L O V U D C T R F
```

SOLUTION PAGE 226

| | |
|---|---|
| ACTOR | FILM |
| AISLE | LIGHTS |
| ARENA | MOVIE |
| ARTS | MUSIC |
| AUDIENCE | OPERA |
| BALCONY | PERFORM |
| BOXES | PLAY |
| BUILDING | POPCORN |
| CINEMA | ROW |
| CONCERT | SCENERY |
| COSTUMES | SET |
| CREW | SHOW |
| CURTAIN | SINGING |
| DANCING | SOUND |
| DARKNESS | STAGE |
| DIRECTOR | TICKET |
| DOOR | USHER |
| DRAMA | WALLS |
| ENTRANCE | WINGS |
| EVENT | |
| EXIT | |

## At the Theater

```
U F U L I G H T S G S E T A
D N S M U S I C N E E G M D
T N H O G X E I Y A M A R D
I Y E E U N C A N A O T O J
C A R D E N I U O M V S F C
K L N R A A D D C E I N R S
E P Y D A R X I L N E E E I
T N I C D E K E A I W M P N
S R T T E N A N B C U T F G
T O R R N A S C E T E B A I
R C E E A E W E S S C S R N
A P C J D N V O A I S L E G
O O N R O T C E R I D L P M
T P O W O H S E X O B A O L
Q L C U R T A I N I U W B I
J S E H S G N I W C T J F F
```

SOLUTION PAGE 226

| | |
|---|---|
| AISLE | KISS |
| BEST MAN | LAW |
| BOUQUET | LOVE |
| CANDLES | MOTHER |
| CHAPEL | MUSIC |
| CHURCH | PRIEST |
| COUPLE | RICE |
| DANCING | RINGS |
| DINNER | RITUALS |
| DRESSES | SHOWER |
| EVENT | SPEECH |
| FAMILY | TOAST |
| FATHER | TUXEDO |
| FOOD | UNION |
| FORMAL | VEIL |
| FRIENDS | VIDEO |
| GARTER | VOWS |
| GIFTS | WHITE |
| GOWN | WIFE |
| GUESTS | |
| HUSBAND | |

## Wedding Day

```
N W O G I F T S H C E E P S
V F I A M W W U L W H I T E
E V C F L U S T S A O T F Q
I V V H E B S S I K U W A L
L F E D A N C I N G J T M H
N O I N U P A T C S R E I P
I O D M T C E M N E L U L R
R D Z S H L E L T S O Q Y I
E F X U P L K R R S V U O E
W V R U S T A G E E E O P S
O C O I R G U L F R N B U T
H C A I E E D X A D I N L S
S M C S S N H Q E M S N I U
R E H T A F D T Q D R M G D
K A S C I I A S O W O O G S
S W O V I D E O P M O Y F K
```

SOLUTION PAGE 226

| | |
|---|---|
| AIR | JET |
| BATTERY | MACHINE |
| BELTS | MECHANIC |
| BLOCK | MOTOR |
| BURN | OIL |
| CAR | PARTS |
| CONVERT | PISTON |
| COOLING | POWER |
| CYLINDER | PROPEL |
| DIESEL | REV |
| DRIVE | ROCKET |
| ELECTRIC | RUN |
| EMISSION | SPEED |
| ENERGY | STEAM |
| ENGINEER | STIRLING |
| EXHAUST | TORQUE |
| FUEL | TURBINE |
| GAS | VALVES |
| GEARS | VEHICLE |
| HEAT | |
| HYDRAULIC | |

# Start Your Engines

```
F D T O K S M O T O R V S H
T E K C O R E E N I G N E A
O E L G R A L P J S Y A X R
R P E Y R E T T A B T R H S
Q S P R C G D I U S Q M A E
U N O T D K R N T R E B U V
E O R R L C A I I C B T S L
T I P A I O R M H L J I T A
C S H C I L U A R D Y H N V
O S H K I B N C J D D C N E
O I A N Z I R H D E S O E H
L M G G C E V I R D T N P I
I E W S W R E N L S E V A C
N U R O O S R E I R A E R L
G K P I E U U P G Y M R T E
W T H L B F I Y B E L T S R
```

SOLUTION PAGE 227

| | |
|---|---|
| BLOCK | NIAGARA |
| CANADA | PARK |
| CASCADE | PLUNGE |
| CATARACT | POOL |
| CHANNEL | RAINBOW |
| CHUTE | RAPID |
| CLIFF | RELAXING |
| CURRENT | RIVER |
| DROP | ROCKS |
| ENERGY | ROMANTIC |
| EROSION | SCENIC |
| FAN | SPLASH |
| FLOW | SPRAY |
| FROZEN | STEEP |
| GOCTA | STREAM |
| GORGE | TALL |
| HAWAII | TIERED |
| HEIGHT | WATER |
| LAKE | WET |
| MIST | |
| NATURE | |

# Waterfall

```
K V A Y R G P L W O L F D V
L R A S A O S A L Z C F Y B
D S F A R R C T R A I I X F
I E I D I G P K R K T L E D
P W D A I E T S S E N C N E
A E U N A D G N I X A L E R
R T B A W A I L E T M M R O
E I C C A C R A A R O J G S
T E U O H S R R F K R Y Y I
A R T Q G A A A R W E U X O
W E H W G C N I O K V N C N
P D G A T Y V N Z C I H I A
Y E I N A F Q B E O R L N T
K N E T U H C O N L X O E U
W W H T T L W W O B V O C R
S Z M I S T P H S A L P S E
```

SOLUTION PAGE 227

| | |
|---|---|
| ABSTRACT | MAPS |
| AIRPORT | MILES |
| ATLAS | MOUNTAIN |
| CAPITALS | NAUTICAL |
| CELESTIAL | PARK |
| CITY | PAVED |
| COMPASS | RAILROAD |
| COUNTY | RELIEF |
| DEGREES | RIVER |
| DESIGN | SCALE |
| DIRT | SCHOOL |
| DISTANCE | SHADED |
| DIVIDED | SOUTH |
| EAST | STREET |
| EQUATOR | SYMBOLS |
| GLOBES | TITLE |
| GRID | TOWN |
| HIGHWAY | TRAVEL |
| HOSPITAL | WEST |
| KEY | |
| LEGEND | |

## On the Map

```
T O W N Y E K R A P A V E D
P A T L A S C H O O L K H E
N G I S E D A O R L I A R D
K P T B X V T C A R T S B A
E Z O H O S P I T A L Y R H
Y L M O U N T A I N K T O S
G X T Z S S A P M O C N T D
R E L I E F L A C I T U A N
Z L D L T C H A W I Z O U E
L A E K D S N I T E T C Q G
E C G I T Y I A G I S Y E E
V S R R E V I R T H P T L L
A T E S L O B M Y S W A C U
R E E L F T R O P R I A C O
T Z S H I D E D I V I D Y I
D I R G O M H T U O S P A M
```

SOLUTION PAGE 227

| | |
|---|---|
| ANIMALS | ORGAN |
| ANTIQUE | PAINTED |
| BENCH | PARK |
| CARNIVAL | PLATFORM |
| CHILDREN | RIDE |
| CIRCLE | RING |
| DIZZY | ROTATE |
| FAIR | ROUND |
| FAMILIES | SEAT |
| FUN | SPIN |
| GALLOPING | TICKET |
| HORSE | TIGERS |
| KIDS | UNICORN |
| LIGHTS | WOODEN |
| LIONS | ZEBRAS |
| MARY POPPINS | |
| MERRY | |
| MIRRORS | |
| MOVEMENT | |
| MUSIC | |
| OLD | |

# Carousel

```
R P O O A B E X T Z D A O L
G T I C K E T C S Y E C M Y
W A N I M A L S R O R R I M
O P B E N C H G E L C R I C
O S R R M N A A G A T S E H
D E P S H E Z L I V N P E M
E A J P T N V L T I E A W F
N T P L L H I O P N R I U A
K H A A V I G P M R D N N I
B O R T G D O I S A L T I R
O R K F O P Y N L C I E C K
P S G O Y R Z G S Q H D O I
Z E B R A S Z N U F C R R D
K F A M I L I E S Z G I N S
F M U S I C D L O A C N V U
T Y E D I R O U N D S G S Z
```

SOLUTION PAGE 227

| | |
|---|---|
| ACTION | HORROR |
| ACTRESS | LEADS |
| AWARDS | LIGHTS |
| BOMB | LOOPING |
| CAMERAS | MAKEUP |
| COLOR | MUSICAL |
| COMEDY | MYSTERY |
| CRITICS | OSCAR |
| CUT | PARTY |
| DOUBLES | PLOT |
| DRAMA | POPCORN |
| DUBBING | PROPS |
| EDITOR | RATINGS |
| EXTRAS | SCRIPT |
| FANS | SEQUEL |
| FEATURE | STARS |
| FLOP | STUNTS |
| FRAMES | THEME |
| GAFFERS | TICKET |
| GENRE | |
| HIT | |

# Silver Screen

```
L E U Q E S L G S B H J S S
E S H J D I P N T R C N R P
X I O R G O A I A O R J L R
T R A H P F U B R T I O C O
R W T C E O C B S I T Z R P
A S O O T R T U L D I M A S
S R G E G W U D N E C U C T
N N F N N A C T R E S S S U
T E K C I T F A A C T I O N
A F L O P T W F M E L C Y T
E M W N O H A N E E F A R S
M R A B O M B R P R R L E D
E O N R L F R A M E S A T A
H L R E D Y R T P I R C S E
T O V R G T N C O M E D Y L
R C X E Y R C P U E K A M Y
```

SOLUTION PAGE 228

55

APPETIZERS

APPLE CRISP

BERRY PIE

BRANDY SNAPS

BROWNIES

CANDY CANES

CARAMEL

CHEESECAKE

CHERRY PIE

CHESTNUTS

CIDER

FUDGE

HARD CANDY

ICE CREAM

KISSES

MACAROONS

MARSHMALLOW

MIXED NUTS

PECAN PIE

PEPPERMINT

PICKLES

PUMPKIN PIE

PUNCH

ROCK CANDY

SHORTBREAD

SODA

SPONGE CAKE

TOFFEE

VEGGIE DIP

# Tasty

```
T R S H O R T B R E A D O S
N E I P Y R R E H C N U P C
I D F W O Y D N A C D R A H
M I X E D N U T S F U D G E R
R C S B V E G G I E D I P E
E R T R A P P E T I Z E R S
P O U A P P L E C R I S P E
P C N N E B S I A A S M U C
E K T D C R N P N C K A M A
P C S Y A O O Y D A I E P K
I A E S N W O R Y R S R K E
C N H N P N R R C A S C I E
K D C A I I A E A M E E N F
L Y S P E E C B N E S C P F
E X V S T S A L E L B I I O
S W O L L A M H S R A M E T
```

SOLUTION PAGE 228

| | |
|---|---|
| ABSORB | ORGAN |
| AERATING | PARSNIP |
| AERIAL | PLANT |
| ANCHOR | POTATO |
| BASE | RUTABAGA |
| BEET | SHOOT |
| BOTANY | SOIL |
| BULB | STORAGE |
| CARROT | SUPPORT |
| CROPS | SURFACE |
| DEEP | TAPROOT |
| DIG | TEA |
| ECOLOGY | THICK |
| FLOWER | TOOTH |
| FOOD | TREE |
| FOREST | TUBER |
| GARDEN | TURNIP |
| GROW | WEED |
| HAIR | YAM |
| HERB | |
| ONION | |

# Roots

```
G Q A W P A C Y D C R O P S
T M E U E N C R I A H N L D
V E N R H C D Q B R O M A R
D B I K A H H S K R O Z N T
K A L D G O O E G O T Y T R
L C E U A R E A R T A N K E
E E I R B G N D E B T A X E
P C E H A E S A B I O T C L
L K A R T T P S U P P O R T
K I O F U A I H T B L B O F
H T O B R M X N T O W O T G
S N U S E U A G G O R O A M
D O N Z W E S Y R P O R D O
O I F O O D T G A H D T E A
P N J E L C I T S E R O F W
A O V R F D P I N R U T Q O
```

SOLUTION PAGE 228

**59**

| | |
|---|---|
| ARCHITECT | JANITOR |
| ARTIST | JUDGE |
| ASTRONAUT | LAWYER |
| AUTHOR | MANAGER |
| BAKER | MARKETING |
| BIOLOGIST | MECHANIC |
| BUTCHER | MUSICIAN |
| CAPTAIN | NURSE |
| CARPENTER | PAINTER |
| CASHIER | PILOT |
| CHEMIST | POSTMAN |
| COACH | SURGEON |
| COUNSELOR | TAILOR |
| DENTIST | WAITRESS |
| DIETITIAN | |
| DOCTOR | |
| DRAFTSMAN | |
| ECONOMIST | |
| EDITOR | |
| GEOLOGIST | |
| HISTORIAN | |

# Get a Job

```
H S R O T C O D E N T I S T
C U A G E O L O G I S T B E
A R R E R O T I N A J S U S
O G T D R O L I A T E I T R
C E I I R G J W I P G M C U
P O S T M A N A R A D O H N
R N T O C U F I O C U N E A
E T C R A T B T T N J O R I
T U A M S H I R S E C C E C
N A R E H O O E I M K E Y I
I N P C I R L S H R A R W S
A O E H E O O S T X E N A U
P R N A R E G A N A M K L M
Z T T N Q D I E T I T I A N
O S E I X T S I M E H C P B
U A R C H I T E C T O L I P
```

SOLUTION PAGE 228

| | |
|---|---|
| ALE | HOPS |
| AMBER | IMPORTED |
| ANHEUSER | INDUSTRY |
| BAR | KEG |
| BEVERAGE | LAGER |
| BOTTLE | LIGHT |
| BRANDS | MILLER |
| BREW | MUG |
| BUD | PABST |
| CAN | PARTY |
| COLD | PILSNER |
| COORS | PINT |
| CRAFT | PRODUCTION |
| DARK | PUB |
| DOMESTIC | REFRESHING |
| DRAFT | SCHLITZ |
| DRINK | STOUT |
| FLAVOR | TAP |
| FOAM | YEAST |
| GRAIN | |
| HEAD | |

## Have a Beer

```
V M P A T O D A E H X S Y R
O X D O E S M R R K D T M A
N V L B K B B E R K R O A A
O V U A E R G A N A C U O N
D D E R E A D I P Q I T F T
T G X L L N R I D M M X L S
G N L Y B D L O P U B L A A
U I I K A S R O O C D I V E
M H D P N D R A F T O G O Y
L S J E H T F A R C M H R E
U E R B E V E R A G E T L G
P R O D U C T I O N S T R D
E F A K S T J O A U T A L E
B E U W E R B C D O I O Y T
B R A Y R G S N B N C C W V
N G B S Z T I L H C S P O H
```

SOLUTION PAGE 229

**63**

BARREL

BLACK

BLOTTER

CAP

CLASSIC

COLOR

CREATE

CURSIVE

DOCUMENT

DRAW

ELEGANT

FANCY

FILL

FLOW

FORMAL

GIFT

GOLD

GRAVITY

HAND

INK

LEAKAGE

LUXURY

MESSY

METAL

NIB

OFFICE

ORNATE

PARKER

PEN

QUALITY

QUILL

SCHOOL

SCRIPT

SHEAFFER

SIGN

STEEL

TIP

TOOL

WELL

WRITE

## Fountain Pens

```
H N B U H U Z J D L S K A W
H W R Y V Z Y U E T U D N R
A L E C S T R E T T O L B I
N U K L I S T B K C A L B T
D X R V L S E C U R S I V E
L U A S Z Y S M B I N D F U
O R P C S H E A F F E R A T
G Y X H P N R E L E G A N T
L L M O T R C O E C P W C P
C L A O E I O R A T Q H Y I
H O I L F T P T K U A M N R
D I R F F O R M A L W E M C
C Z O N I Y W L G I F T R S
W H G P A P I O E R O L O C
J I Q L A T E M L L I U Q G
S K G X Y C E N H F Q E P L
```

SOLUTION PAGE 229

# Crossword Puzzles

## ACROSS

1. Old radio's ___ 'n' Andy
5. Passports, for example: Abbr.
8. Earring's place
12. Chair or sofa
13. Lion sign
14. Former Indiana senator Bayh
15. ___ boy!
16. PC linking system
17. Performed an aria
18. Hershey competitor
20. Theater walkway
22. Brain-wave test, briefly
23. *Norma* ___
24. Tail motion
27. Rebel Turner
29. Monument Valley features
33. A sister of Zsa Zsa
34. ___ Palmas, Spain
36. Perform on a stage
37. Reduced, as pain
40. 1960s conflict site, for short
42. Perfect Olympics score
43. Actor Stephen of *The Crying Game*
45. Half an umlaut
47. Suddenly stop, as an engine
49. Hangmen's ropes
53. "___ a Lady" (Tom Jones hit)
54. Honest president
56. Aviation-related prefix
57. Sharpen, as a knife
58. Univ. dorm supervisors
59. Pierce with a fork
60. Red ___ (cinnamon candies)
61. Is it Miss or ___?
62. Soviet news source

## DOWN

1. Wise ___ owl
2. Measure (out)
3. Feed bag fill
4. Michigan or Minnesota
5. Lawbreaking
6. Narcs' agcy.
7. Submarine detector
8. Apartment dweller
9. Zero-shaped
10. Cause of one's undoing
11. Subj. including grammar
19. Football Hall of Famer Dawson
21. "___ Woman" (Reddy song)
24. Pint-sized
25. Actress Gardner
26. Exxon product
28. Catch some rays
30. Fri. follower
31. Perfect tennis serve

# Crossword Puzzle 1

SOLUTION PAGE 230

32. Train depot: Abbr.
35. Blue feeling
38. Cleans the blackboard
39. ___ Monte (food giant)
41. Cow word
44. Security feature
46. Raise a glass to

47. Get lost, fly!
48. Camper's shelter
50. ___ good example
51. Time periods
52. Blubbers
53. Quiet down!
55. High-jumper's hurdle

## ACROSS

1. ___ fun at (ridicule)
5. Edinburgh native
9. ABBA's "Mamma ___"
12. Barely manages, with "out"
13. Task list heading
14. ___ in the bag
15. Pecan and pumpkin
16. Pink, as cheeks
17. Educ. institution
18. Makes very happy
20. Sore all over
21. Talk, talk, talk
22. *Oedipus* ___
24. Deep gorge
27. Heredity-related
31. School transportation
32. Like an eagle in flight
34. Hosp. area for emergency cases
35. Like a clear night sky
37. Sprinted
39. Minister, slangily
40. So ___, so good
41. Detroit products
44. Truman who wrote *Breakfast at Tiffany's*
47. Chimp or gorilla
48. What the "ten" of "hang ten" refers to
50. ___ *Lisa*
52. Game show host Sajak
53. Litter weakling
54. Circle segments
55. Like octogenarians
56. Music, ballet, sculpture, etc.
57. Polio vaccine developer

## DOWN

1. Liven (up)
2. Muskogee native
3. On an even ___ (stable)
4. School papers
5. Throat ailment
6. Dove or love murmurs
7. Pigs out (on), briefly
8. Kind of poodle
9. Various: Abbr.
10. Something to scratch
11. Like a fireplace floor
19. Tex-Mex snack
20. Logger's tool
22. NBA official
23. Lure into crime
24. *60 Minutes* airer
25. Quonset ___
26. Smart ___ whip
27. "I ___ You Babe"
28. ___ Tac (breath freshener)
29. Skater's surface
30. What a cow chews
33. Actress Tyler of *Armageddon*

# Crossword Puzzle 2

SOLUTION PAGE 230

36. Train lines: Abbr.
38. Inviting smells
40. Abstains from eating
41. Aria da ___
42. Be ___ ...: "Help me"
43. AARP part: Abbr.
44. Coin with Lincoln's profile

45. When said three times, a 1970 war film
46. SASE, e.g.
48. Syllable before "la la"
49. First word of the Lord's Prayer
51. Query

## ACROSS

1. Medical insurance abbr.
4. PC panic button
7. ___ Rushmore
12. Forbid
13. Wine tasting?
14. Jazz great Shaw
15. Poor movie rating
17. When it ___, it pours
18. Garment bottom
19. Shoreline irregularity
20. Secret stash
23. Eggy drink
24. GI entertainment sponsor
25. Prefix with bytes or bucks
28. Jane Austen classic
32. Tavern
33. Holy one
35. What you breathe
36. Mimicked
38. Crossword hint
39. Paranormal showman Geller
40. Come again?
42. Wielded authority
44. Title colonel in a 1960s sitcom
47. Afternoons and evenings, briefly
48. Tennis champ Chris
49. Gets one's bearings
53. Physics Nobelist Enrico
54. Believe it or ___!
55. Just great
56. Courtroom event
57. Poem of tribute
58. No. on a transcript

## DOWN

1. *Entourage* network
2. A ___ for All Seasons
3. Long-distance number starter
4. Holds in high regard
5. Thailand's former name
6. EMT's forte
7. Nintendo's Super ___ Bros.
8. Juice source
9. Elec. company
10. Number of Muses
11. Trial run
16. Quiet!
20. Havana's home
21. Quickly!, on an order
22. Apple leftover
23. Half of Mork's farewell
26. "Hurting ___ Other" (The Carpenters)
27. Baseball great Hodges
29. Badly claw
30. Oozy ground
31. Like a dust bowl
34. Orkin target
37. Greg's sitcom partner
41. ___ we meet again

# Crossword Puzzle 3

SOLUTION PAGE 230

43. ___ it or lose it
44. Lift with effort
45. Partner of "done with"
46. Halliwell of the Spice Girls
47. Cow poke?
49. Lennon's widow Yoko
50. Racehorse, slangily

51. First-rate
52. Calypso cousin

## ACROSS

1. Is able to
4. PC program, briefly
7. Staircase part
11. Troop entertainment sponsor: Abbr.
12. Banister
14. Oompah instrument
15. Put down, in the 'hood
16. Quote authoritatively
17. Dear ___
18. Cut off
20. Attempts
22. Bartender's requests, maybe
23. Attila, for one
24. Wander aimlessly
27. Prohibition
28. Nightwear, briefly
31. Detroit labor org.
32. Golden calf et al.
34. Antique auto
35. Gridiron grp.
36. Morning drops
37. 2000 "Subway Series" losers
38. Small child
39. Fed. purchasing group
41. Nonpoetic writing
43. Assumed name
46. Sound of distress
47. Amount between all and none
49. *Play It Again, ___*
51. Bush adviser Karl
52. It marches on
53. ___ *Got a Secret*
54. Colored eye part
55. Place for a napkin
56. Gave dinner

## DOWN

1. What cows chew
2. Without warranties
3. Prominent Durante feature
4. Followed a curved path
5. Twosomes
6. Deep hole
7. Spot on a tie, say
8. Toothpaste holder
9. Flows out
10. Foot the bill
13. Deadly
19. ___ and vigor
21. Baseball scores
24. Campaign (for)
25. Stumblebum
26. Leatherworker's puncher
27. Violist's need
28. Post- opposite
29. Boeing 747, e.g.
30. Shipwreck signal
32. They're exchanged at the altar
33. Dislike with a passion
37. Chiang ___ (Thai city)

# Crossword Puzzle 4

SOLUTION PAGE 230

38. Musical sounds
39. Beta's follower
40. Insomniac's need
41. Impoverished
42. Sitar master Shankar
44. ___ I care!
45. Put away for a rainy day

46. Hosp. scan
48. Salad dressing ingredient
50. Club ___ resort

## ACROSS

1. No. on a bank statement
5. School of thought
8. Sandwich initials
11. 60 minutes
12. Wintry
13. Inauguration declaration
14. Allot, with "out"
15. Electrically charged atom
16. Reverse, as an action
17. Garden of ___
18. Treaty
20. Not made up
23. Arm joint
27. Idiosyncrasy
30. Approves
31. The "L" of XXL
32. Where telecommuters work
34. Word of warning
35. Barton of the Red Cross
36. PETA peeve
37. *Waking ___ Devine* (1998 film)
38. From days of yore
39. One-named New Age vocalist
41. Egg on
43. Give at no charge, as a hotel room
47. Sushi bar soup
50. Rioting group
52. Swedish furniture retailer
53. "Go Tell ___ the Mountain"
54. Cook, as bacon
55. Pickle herb
56. It may be put out to pasture
57. Fannie ___ (federal mortgage agency)
58. Complete collections

## DOWN

1. Alas
2. For both sexes
3. Adorable
4. Lott of Mississippi
5. Three, on a sundial
6. Monkey Trial name
7. Gabby bird
8. Make taboo
9. Inc. alternative
10. However, informally
13. Wanted felon
19. Crunchy vegetable
21. *Everybody Loves Raymond* star
22. Tiny Tim played one
24. Raisin ___ (cereal)
25. Folklore meanie
26. Unwanted lawn growth
27. Stuffed tortilla
28. ___ be a cold day in...
29. Punched-out part of a paper ballot
33. Eugene's state

# Crossword Puzzle 5

SOLUTION PAGE 231

34. Burger roll
36. Bogart's hat
40. Corrosive liquids
42. Car radio button
44. 1930s migrant
45. Liquefy
46. Best buds

47. What an MC wears
48. Who am ___ judge?
49. Miss Piggy, e.g.
51. See ya

## ACROSS

1. Dose amt.
4. Talk online
8. Pot-bellied critter
11. Wednesday's child is full of it
12. Skillfully
13. ___ Major (constellation)
14. ___ Gang comedies
15. Betsy or Diana
16. Showy display
17. Baseball's Bambino
19. Partner of aahs
21. Chinese cooking vessel
23. Poverty-stricken
26. Made a getaway
30. Pub perch
32. Half a quartet
33. "___ Are My Sunshine"
35. Three: Prefix
36. City-related
39. Accumulated
42. Went out, as the tide
44. Engine additive letters
45. Follow, as advice
47. "Battle ___ of the Republic"
50. "Round and Round" singer Perry
53. Sidewalk eatery
55. Look through the crosshairs
57. Are you coming ___ not?
58. Ken or Lena
59. Nova subj.
60. Mom's mate
61. Deli breads
62. Voodoo doctor's doing

## DOWN

1. A pair
2. Like a lime
3. Llama country
4. Server at a drive-in
5. *Big Love* airer
6. ___ -ran: loser
7. Boxing's "Iron Mike"
8. Paid player
9. Doctrine: Suffix
10. Noticeable opening
13. Unexpected sports outcome
18. Up, up, and away defunct flier
20. For ___ a jolly good...
22. Door opener
24. Periods
25. Olden times
26. University URL ending
27. Be glad to
28. Ty or Lee J.
29. ___ one-eighty
31. Pot's top
34. Hesitant sounds
37. Really hate
38. Previously named
40. Greek metropolis

# Crossword Puzzle 6

SOLUTION PAGE 231

41. Undercover agent
43. Interior designer's concern
46. Tyne of *Cagney & Lacey*
48. Alan Alda series
49. Delightful
50. Scotland Yard div.
51. *Cat ___ Hot Tin Roof*

52. Stylish, 1960s-style
54. What foolishness!
56. Blender setting

## ACROSS

1. Game show hosts: Abbr.
4. Plays a part
8. 300 in old Rome
11. Tell everyone
13. Breakfast restaurant chain
14. English lavatory
15. Excellent rating
16. Distance divided by time
17. Big fuss
18. Stainless metal
20. Chaney of old films
21. Kind of rally or talk
22. Just do it sloganeer
24. Explosive ltrs.
26. Bullring "Bravo!"
29. Vintners' vessels
31. Appeal to God
34. Hair-setting item
36. Steep-roofed house
38. Chicken cordon ___
39. Great Salt ___
41. Interest amt.
42. Grand Hotel studio
44. Not a ___ out of you!:
    "Shh!"
46. Top flier
48. Rink surface
50. Arranges by type
54. Panel truck
55. Not wild
57. Hammer or saw
58. Say no, with "out"
59. Overhead transportation
60. Chinese: Prefix
61. Figs.
62. Passed along
63. Relay race part

## DOWN

1. Corp. execs' degrees
2. Blood blockage
3. Mentally fit
4. Breathable stuff
5. Alpine dwelling
6. Oz canine
7. Paid out
8. Nonsense
9. Morse's creation
10. Hen pen
12. I've ___ had!
19. Not taped
23. Bush adviser Rove
25. *All Things Considered*
    network
26. Sun or moon, to bards
27. Online chuckle
28. Tungsten and tellurium
30. For goodness' ___!
32. Rambler mfr.
33. You ain't seen nothin' ___!
35. Big galoot
37. Doctors' charges
40. Tarzan, for one

# Crossword Puzzle 7

SOLUTION PAGE 231

43. Catchers' gloves
45. Stew holders
46. Bell-ringing cosmetics company
47. Crime chief
49. Give a darn
51. Agitate

52. Dial sound
53. Wade through mud
56. Ambulance worker, for short

## ACROSS

1. Classic Pontiac muscle cars
5. Sized up visually
9. College transcript no.
12. Cry of anticipation
13. 1920s–1940s art style
14. Certain retriever, briefly
15. Use a wrecking ball on
16. From ___: completely
17. Poet's planet
18. Gives in
20. Room to maneuver
22. Connected to the Internet
24. Kind of symbol
27. Hair goo
28. Mary had a little one
32. Cat's cry
34. Coll. dorm VIPs
36. Fat used in candle making
37. Mama's partner
38. Mom's month
40. Homophone for new
41. Kathmandu resident
44. John, Paul, George, or Ringo
47. Envelope enclosure
52. Treater's pickup
53. Shoestring
55. Maui feast
56. Internet address, briefly
57. Cast-___ stomach
58. Copier input: Abbr.
59. Stealthy
60. Mail-chute opening
61. Pantheon members

## DOWN

1. Bloody
2. Southeast Asian cuisine
3. Trickle
4. Writer/illustrator Silverstein
5. Lou Grant portrayer
6. Are we having fun ___?
7. Food-poisoning bacteria
8. Egg carton count
9. Post-sunset effect
10. Prefix with legal
11. Dear advice giver
19. Follow everywhere
21. Morays, e.g.
23. Peruvian beast
24. Ref's cousin
25. Unimpressive brain size
26. Badge wearer
29. Jul. follower
30. Fraternity members
31. Appliance meas.
33. Privation
35. Noteworthy
39. Yang's counterpart
42. ___ Island (immigrants' site)
43. Oyster's prize
44. AC measures
45. "Duke of ___" (1962 hit)

# Crossword Puzzle 8

SOLUTION PAGE 231

46. With adroitness
48. Trudge through the mire
49. Currency on the Continent
50. Police assault
51. Actions on heartstrings and pant legs
54. Dovish sound

## ACROSS

1. Hardly neatniks
5. ___ *a Teenage Werewolf*
9. Roast hosts, for short
12. Going ___ (bickering)
13. Verb accompanier
14. Pirate's assent
15. Sammy with three 60-homer seasons
16. Roman robe
17. Recipe abbreviation
18. Fido's warning
20. Fictional Butler
22. Mineo of *Exodus*
25. Mal de mer symptom
28. Tire pressure letters
29. ___ *of Green Gables*
30. Feed, as pigs
34. Fills with wonder
36. Envy or sloth
37. Father
38. List from a waiter
39. "___ Long Way to Tipperary"
41. Pres. Coolidge
42. Self-___ (pride)
44. Carrier to Amsterdam
45. Tongue's sense
48. Caustic substance
50. ___ thumbs: clumsy
51. Yahtzee pieces

54. Springsteen's nickname, with "the"
58. Architect I.M. ___
59. Puts on TV
60. Make cookies
61. Bilko or Friday: Abbr.
62. Louse eggs
63. Omit

## DOWN

1. Joad and Kettle
2. Lance of the bench
3. USO show audience
4. Party for men
5. On the way
6. Go a-courting
7. Mo. before Labor Day
8. Drum type
9. G'day, ___!
10. Dermatologist's removal
11. Labor Day mo.
19. Genetic carrier
21. Padlock holder
22. Unsolicited email
23. ...___ forgive those who trespass...
24. Bank's property claim
26. Join forces
27. Lacking meaning
31. Be deficient in
32. Down Under gemstone
33. Tree in Miami

# Crossword Puzzle 9

SOLUTION PAGE 232

35. Bird-feeder block
40. TV's *Judging* ___
43. Alternative to a station wagon or convertible
45. Spigots
46. Break ___!
47. Thin cut

49. Recedes, as the tide
52. Caesar's three
53. Old PC component
55. Acorn maker
56. Hit the slopes
57. Autumn mo.

## ACROSS

1. ___ and now
5. ___ Na Na
8. Twirl
12. Man in Eden
13. May and June: Abbr.
14. ___-Cola
15. Local bond, familiarly
16. Two-by-two vessel
17. Give the thumbs-up
18. Gretzky's grp.
20. Eyeglass part
21. Sex ___
24. Puddle gunk
26. Mama Judd
27. Fix illegally
28. Small amount
31. Chip go-with
32. *The Mary Tyler Moore Show* spin-off
34. Post-op locale
35. 1999 and 2000: Abbr.
36. Wall Street index, with "the"
37. Sans clothing
39. Part of a gearwheel
40. Look up to
41. Peter the Great, for one
44. China's Chairman ___
45. Missing a deadline
46. ___ Guevara
48. Small screen award
52. Don't count ___!
53. Try to get elected
54. Born and ___
55. Le Pew of cartoons
56. Balance sheet abbr.
57. Helps

## DOWN

1. Sandwich meat
2. University web address suffix
3. Fled the scene
4. *8 Mile* rapper
5. Wee
6. Vert. opposite
7. Pose a question
8. Give a tongue-lashing
9. Place for a pig?
10. Sammy Davis Jr.'s "Yes ___"
11. Thumbs-down votes
19. Bob or beehive
21. Raggedy doll
22. Duo
23. Boston ___
24. Prefix with shipman
25. Where Idi Amin ruled
27. Use the oars
28. Hawaiian carving
29. Skillful server on the court
30. Fellow, slangily
33. Greedy type
38. One-celled protozoan
39. Largest Greek island
40. Revise

# Crossword Puzzle 10

SOLUTION PAGE 232

41. Horse hoof sound

42. Writer Grey

43. Eagerly expecting

46. "When Doves ___" (Prince)

47. Primitive home

49. Hosp. test

50. Club ___ (resort)

51. Football gains: Abbr.

## ACROSS

1. Defective firecracker
4. Rowing equipment
8. Solar-system center
11. Words of surprise
13. Agonize (over)
14. Storekeeper in *The Simpsons*
15. Shoreline indentation
16. Cry of unveiling
17. Hither and ___
18. Shave, as sheep
20. Cranberry-growing site
21. Carry-___ (small pieces of luggage)
22. Watch face
24. Thesaurus listing: Abbr.
26. Tai ___ (exercise method)
29. Aviated
31. Diplomatic quality
34. Richly decorated
36. Mitchell of NBC News
38. HS junior's exam
39. TV's "Warrior Princess"
41. Height: Abbr.
42. Bag-like structure
44. Pants parts
46. Revolutionist Guevara
48. Have in hand
50. Hide for future use
54. Solo in Star Wars
55. Articulated
57. Abruptly dismissed
58. Question's opposite: Abbr.
59. Singer Turner
60. Lahr or Parks
61. JFK's predecessor
62. Messy dresser
63. Restroom, informally

## DOWN

1. Physicians, briefly
2. This looks bad
3. Winged peace symbol
4. Frequently, to Frost
5. Good for farming
6. Change the decor of
7. Does' mates
8. Japanese farewell
9. "When You Wish ___ a Star"
10. Women in habits
12. Noggin
19. Break in relations
23. Trebek of *Jeopardy!*
25. Since Jan. 1
26. Radar gun aimer
27. *48* ___ (Nick Nolte film)
28. Looking at it one way
30. Grow dim
32. Cartoon frame
33. "I tawt I taw a puddy ___!"
35. ___ standstill (motionless)
37. Pesters persistently

# Crossword Puzzle 11

SOLUTION PAGE 232

40. Pacific weather phenomenon
43. Prices
45. Attack with a knife
46. Neighbor of Niger
47. Something to shake with
49. Cry out

51. Beverly Hills Cop character Foley
52. Will be, in a Doris Day song
53. Modern RCA offering
56. Small amount, as of hair cream

## ACROSS

1. Hollywood heartthrob Pitt
5. Golfing standard
8. Managed care grps.
12. Film part
13. Common Father's Day gift
14. Dad's sister
15. ___ boy! ("Nice going!")
16. Early hrs.
17. Luge, for one
18. Winter neckwear
20. Hearing and sight
22. Comedian Bernie
24. ___ Aviv
25. In ___ (behind)
29. Overalls material
33. Humble home
34. Wilder's ___ *Town*
36. One ___ kind
37. Something to lend or bend
40. North Star
43. Beanie
45. ___ appétit!
46. Mexican snacks
49. Calls a spade a thpade
53. Oliver Twist's request
54. Singing group ___ Na Na
56. Castle encircler
57. Has dinner
58. Comic Conway
59. Friend in war
60. ___ and wherefores
61. Hot springs site
62. Be defeated

## DOWN

1. Swimsuit tops
2. Campus mil. program
3. ___ Vista (former search engine)
4. Oh, what am I to do?
5. Sch. org.
6. Points (at)
7. Start over button
8. Give a hard time
9. Stubborn animal
10. Singletons
11. Pt. of EST
19. Gov't air-safety org.
21. Flanders of *The Simpsons*
23. ___ -Magnon man
25. Successful solver's shout
26. Seek office
27. US 1, for one
28. Have dinner
30. Neither hide ___ hair
31. ___ *Were King*
32. Pas' partners
35. Lowe or Reiner
38. Passwords provide it
39. Word of cheer
41. Texter's guffaw
42. Orwell's ___ *Farm*
44. Fence supports

# Crossword Puzzle 12

SOLUTION PAGE 232

46. Word-wise Webster
47. Superficially cultured
48. Use UPS, e.g.
50. Unaccompanied performance
51. Buddies
52. Eyelid trouble

53. Kitten's plaint
55. Doctors' grp.

## ACROSS

1. Roadies carry them
5. Nonstick cooking spray
8. Old space station
11. NASCAR's Yarborough
12. Thurman of *The Avengers*
13. Surrender, as land
14. "___ Fire": Springsteen hit
15. Letters between K and O
16. Like deserts
17. Spiderlike bug
20. Plopped (down)
21. Home of the Braves: Abbr.
22. Pal in Paris
25. 1960s Chinese chairman
27. Bother persistently
31. New Balance competitor
33. Gosh, it's cold!
35. Very long story
36. Actress Close
38. Slangy wonderful
40. Corn holder
41. New England fish
43. No ___ (Chinese menu phrase)
45. Exotic destinations
52. Barbecue offerings
53. New Deal agcy.
54. Cheesy fiction
55. Lake near Niagara Falls
56. Children's game
57. Wry Bombeck

58. ___ Moines
59. Steady as ___ goes
60. Piggy bank opening

## DOWN

1. Citric ___
2. Bear with cold porridge
3. Trudge (along)
4. Puts in the mail
5. Soda can feature
6. Bullets and such
7. Food from heaven
8. A ___ pittance
9. Got it, man
10. Johnny Bench's team
13. Maria of the Met
18. Sweet potato cousin
19. Communications conglomerate
22. *Hulk* director Lee
23. $1,000,000, for short
24. Prez after Harry
26. Hockey Hall of Famer Bobby
28. Tic-toe connection
29. "Long, Long ___"
30. Bill at the bar
32. Crate up
34. Rioting
37. Presently
39. High-speed connection
42. Pub projectiles
44. Stares open-mouthed

# Crossword Puzzle 13

| 1 | 2 | 3 | 4 | ■ | 5 | 6 | 7 | ■ | 8 | 9 | 10 |
|---|---|---|---|---|---|---|---|---|---|---|---|
| 11 | | | | ■ | 12 | | | 13 | | | |
| 14 | | | | ■ | 15 | | | 16 | | | |
| 17 | | | | 18 | | | 19 | | | | |
| ■ | ■ | ■ | 20 | | | ■ | 21 | | | ■ | ■ |
| 22 | 23 | 24 | ■ | 25 | | 26 | ■ | 27 | | 28 | 29 | 30 |
| 31 | | | 32 | ■ | 33 | | 34 | ■ | 35 | | | |
| 36 | | | | 37 | ■ | 38 | | 39 | ■ | 40 | | |
| ■ | ■ | ■ | 41 | | 42 | ■ | 43 | | 44 | ■ | ■ | ■ |
| 45 | 46 | 47 | | | | 48 | | | | 49 | 50 | 51 |
| 52 | | | | ■ | 53 | | | ■ | 54 | | | |
| 55 | | | | ■ | 56 | | | ■ | 57 | | | |
| 58 | | | ■ | 59 | | | ■ | 60 | | | |

SOLUTION PAGE 233

45. Flintstone fellow
46. Million or billion suffix
47. Stats for sluggers
48. Right on!
49. Barbell rep
50. Tickle Me ___
51. Falling-out

## ACROSS

1. Art ___ (1920s–1930s style)
5. Narrow opening
9. Pts. of tons
12. Pearl Harbor's site
13. Louise or Turner
14. Debt acknowledgment
15. What time ___ ?
16. *30 Rock* costar Baldwin
17. Vehicle with sliding doors
18. Ad to lure you in
20. Choirs may stand on them
22. Cavern
24. Co. alternative
27. The ___ State (Idaho)
28. Biblical ark builder
32. Nickel or dime
34. Martin Sheen, to Charlie
36. It has its ups and downs
37. Promo recording
38. Attention-getting call
40. Wield an axe
41. I beg of you
44. Come into view
47. In one piece
52. *The Bell* ___ (Sylvia Plath book)
53. Pinocchio, at times
55. Prefix meaning "same"
56. From ___ Z
57. Skin woe
58. Bit of chicanery
59. Crosses (out)
60. Tail movements
61. Tourists' aids

## DOWN

1. ___ -yourself kit
2. "___ on Down the Road"
3. ___ Pet (cultivatable gift)
4. The triple in a triple play
5. Had the top role (in)
6. ___ *Abner*
7. Nonreactive, as some gases
8. Silently understood
9. Walk the earth
10. Part of an old English Christmas feast
11. Soaks up rays
19. ___ foo yung
21. PlayStation maker
23. Nebraska's first capital
24. Digital readout, initially
25. Pedal digit
26. Poorly lit
29. Amazed audience utterance
30. Sailor's "yes"
31. ___ do you do?
33. Slangy denial
35. Wishes
39. Tokyo dough
42. Bochco TV drama
43. *Fear of Fifty* writer Jong
44. Stronger than dirt sloganeer

# Crossword Puzzle 14

SOLUTION PAGE 233

45. Hors d'oeuvre spread
46. Major leaguers
48. Semester
49. Light greenish blue
50. Cutting edge
51. Knots

54. *The Ice Storm* director ___ Lee

## ACROSS

1. Ho ___ Minh
4. ...man ___ mouse?
7. Dracula portrayer Lugosi
11. Not in the office
12. Biblical wise men
14. Ball game delayer
15. Decreased
17. ___ *Almighty* (2007 film)
18. Calligrapher's liquid
19. Movie theater
21. Mixes
24. Alan of *Shane*
25. Swine
26. China, Japan, etc.
29. Half a bray
30. Singer Ronstadt
31. Oinker
33. Leaves high and dry
35. Doozy
36. It's said with a sigh
37. Ambulance sound
38. Motley, as an army
41. Chinese Chairman ___
42. Death notice for short
43. Students
48. Steeple feature
49. Fitzgerald of jazz
50. Snake that squeezes its prey
51. Model Macpherson
52. *Real ___ Don't Eat Quiche*
53. Monty Python airer

## DOWN

1. Rank below general: Abbr.
2. Shade of color
3. The "I" in TGIF
4. Signs of things to come
5. ___ and file
6. Get better, as wine
7. Starr of the comics
8. Roof part
9. Neeson of *Kinsey*
10. Kournikova of tennis
13. What bouncers check
16. Knighted ones
20. Start of an invention
21. Quiet, please!
22. Tot's "piggies"
23. This is the thanks ___?
24. Touches down
26. Wangle
27. Cowboy boot attachment
28. Linoleum alternative
30. Tra-___
32. Rifle or revolver
34. Baby's noisemaker
35. MGM symbol
37. Brand of wrap
38. Justice's attire
39. One slain by Cain
40. Fish's breathing organ
41. Boy or man
44. Nightmare street of film
45. Outward flow

# Crossword Puzzle 15

SOLUTION PAGE 233

46. Filch
47. Possum's pouch

## ACROSS

1. Hoover's org.
4. ___ Loma, Calif.
8. Prefix with dextrous
12. All you ___ eat
13. Dress
14. Mortgage, for example
15. PC screen
16. ___ out? (pet's choice)
17. Manor master
18. "Sweet Caroline" singer
21. I-70, e.g.
22. Partner of hem
23. Just ___! ("Hold on!")
25. Govt. prosecutors
26. Biol. or chem.
29. Nuclear explosion aftermath
33. Animal in the house
34. ___ deco
35. Chatters
36. See ___ care!
37. Larry King employer
38. Carnival treat
43. The ___ Ranger
44. Pants-on-fire person
45. Disconsolate
47. Oyster relative
48. Would you care for anything ___?
49. Where surgeons work: Abbr.
50. Cub Scout groups
51. Straphanger's lack
52. Live from NY show

## DOWN

1. Govt. media watchdog
2. Farm structure
3. Bank accrual
4. Limber
5. Hit the runway
6. *Star Trek: TNG* counselor Deanna
7. Isaac's father
8. Let happen
9. Apollo 11 destination
10. Poet
11. Mich. neighbor
19. Poison ivy symptom
20. Fem.'s opposite
23. Piece of band equipment
24. Instigate litigation
25. "j" topper
26. Blankety-blank ones
27. Soup order
28. Co. photo badges, e.g.
30. Huck's craft
31. Baltimore nine
32. Nashville's Loretta
36. Agenda details
37. Insertion mark
38. Old king of rhyme
39. Chestnuts roasting ___ open fire

# Crossword Puzzle 16

SOLUTION PAGE 233

40. Christie's *Death on the* ___
41. House in Spain
42. Kitten's plaything
43. Watch display, for short
46. Cable modem alternative, briefly

## ACROSS

1. Prom night transportation
5. Scannable mdse. bars
8. Cupid's mo.
11. Apple debut of 1998
12. Comic Caesar
13. Edison's middle name
14. Mixed breed
15. Billy Joel's "Tell ___ about It"
16. Billiards sticks
17. On dry land
19. Do unto ___ ...
21. ___ for the course
22. Cry to a calf
23. Seattle ballplayer
27. Lesson from Aesop
31. Sixth sense letters
32. ER staffers
34. Part of a milit. address
35. "The sky's the ___!"
38. Overlook's offering
41. Director's call
43. Tint
44. Reduce in rank
47. Speechified
51. Victor's cry
52. Eagles' org.
54. Prefix meaning "trillion"
55. Catholic ritual
56. ___ -la-la
57. Deposited
58. ___ -Caps (Nestlé candy)
59. Not vert.
60. 1978 Village People hit

## DOWN

1. Peru's largest city
2. Radio host Don
3. Algebra and trig
4. Eight-armed creatures
5. Led down the aisle
6. Mincemeat dessert
7. PC storage medium
8. Chimney duct
9. ...happily ___ after
10. Lowest voice
13. Sound of a sneeze
18. Competed politically
20. Adventure hero Swift
23. Gibson or Blanc
24. Do ___ say, not...
25. 33 or 45, e.g.
26. They have Xings
28. *Norma* ___ (Sally Field film)
29. Mo. before May
30. Silver-screen star Myrna
33. Learned one
36. Desktop pictures
37. Egypt's King ___
39. Where Switz. is
40. With every hair in place
42. Sophomore's grade
44. Lowers, as a light

# Crossword Puzzle 17

SOLUTION PAGE 234

45. McGregor of *Moulin Rouge!*
46. Soup with sushi
48. Go, ___!
49. Hockey star Lindros
50. Absurdist art movement
53. To's reverse

## ACROSS

1. It might say WELCOME
4. Wastes, in mob slang
8. Ladder rung
12. Bread for a ham sandwich
13. "___ Ha'i" (*South Pacific* song)
14. Early late-night host
15. Poster paints
17. Palo ___, Calif.
18. Hurricane centers
19. Use an iron
20. Sail holders
23. Tortoise's race opponent
25. I can't believe ___ the whole thing!
26. Trig term
27. Gun rights org.
30. Pleasantly concise
33. 180° from NNE
34. Tetra- doubled
35. Radio letters
36. Frat recruiting event
37. Actress Glenn
38. Modern surgical tool
41. Great Caesar's ghost!
43. Landers and Sothern
44. Sitcom segments
48. Funny sketch
49. Bygone days
50. Exerciser's unit
51. Maple syrup fluids
52. Poker starter
53. Cloud backdrop

## DOWN

1. *The A-Team* star
2. Favorable vote
3. Pro ___ : for now
4. Follows directions
5. Price of a ride
6. Short-lived success
7. Lisa, to Bart Simpson
8. Extra tire
9. A fisherman may spin one
10. Breaks bread
11. Major leaguers
16. Actor Ustinov
19. White House VIP
20. Young lady
21. Oohs' companions
22. Store (away)
24. Shave-haircut link
26. Anatomical pouches
27. Pixar fish
28. Football officials
29. Look ___ when I'm talking to you!
31. ___ de France
32. Ralph ___ Emerson
36. Catches one's breath
37. Hindu social division
38. Scottish girl
39. Paul who wrote "My Way"

# Crossword Puzzle 18

SOLUTION PAGE 234

40. Scissors cut
42. Essential meaning
44. Clean Air Act org.
45. Welby and Kildare: Abbr.
46. Mouse hater's cry
47. Finder of secrets

## ACROSS

1. Singer Kristofferson
5. Level out the lawn
8. They may be parallel or uneven
12. "___ Rock" (Simon & Garfunkel hit)
13. Mai ___ (tropical drink)
14. Wait just ___!
15. December 24 and 31
16. Part of CST
17. Express relief
18. Dog docs
19. Radiator emanation
21. Kennel sound
24. Arctic barkers
28. Trio before O
31. Clues, to a detective
34. Icky, sticky stuff
35. Wide shoe spec
36. Wigwam relative
37. Negotiator with GM
38. Part of TGIF: Abbr.
39. Make changes to
40. McMahon and Sullivan
41. Voice below alto
43. Quart divs.
45. Gorbachev was its last leader: Abbr.
48. Fizzling-out sound
52. Small pieces
55. Sound of a punch
57. That's ___! ("Not true!")
58. ___ of arms
59. Big part of an elephant
60. Word repeated after "Que" in a song
61. Bombs that don't explode
62. Lacking moisture
63. Military lunchroom

## DOWN

1. Ukraine's capital
2. Glowing review
3. *How ___ Your Mother*: CBS sitcom
4. Smart-mouthed
5. Everest and St. Helens
6. Courtroom pledge
7. Ample, as a doorway
8. Moisten while cooking
9. Do ___ say, not...
10. Alternative to unleaded (abbr.)
11. Jr. high, e.g.
20. State with confidence
22. Sacrificial sites
23. Orange throwaway
25. Flu-like symptoms
26. Put bullets in
27. Spreads seed
28. Not right
29. A ___ pittance: very little
30. Opposite of "ja"

# Crossword Puzzle 19

SOLUTION PAGE 234

32. It may have two BRs
33. Not shallow
42. Removes from office
44. Involuntary twitch
46. Risked a ticket
47. Crowd noise
49. Turn tail

50. Needle-bearing trees
51. 4:00 socials
52. String after A
53. Promissory initials
54. Itsy bit
56. Twisted, as humor

## ACROSS

1. Mississippi's Trent
5. Just ___ thought!
8. Purchase offers
12. French franc successor
13. Certain boxing win, for short
14. Salt Lake state
15. The Rolling Stones' "Time ___ My Side"
16. Counterpart of long.
17. Chichi
18. Bad mark
20. MetLife competitor
22. Decorative vessel
23. Opposite NNW
24. ___ stone (hieroglyphic key)
28. Parisian pancake
32. I smell ___!
33. "___ Maria"
35. Mr. Flintstone
36. Cat chat
38. Helps out
40. Suffix with cash, cloth, or hotel
42. ___ Francisco
43. Carbo-loader's fare
45. 2000 candidate
49. Surprise "from the blue"
50. 24 hours
52. Online marketplace
53. Zero, on a court
54. Who ___ we kidding?
55. Actor's part
56. ___ she blows!
57. Dispose of
58. Palm reader, e.g.

## DOWN

1. Hawaiian garlands
2. Get rid of
3. *Star Trek: TNG* counselor Deanna
4. Enunciation challenge
5. Home of the Braves
6. Caribbean music
7. Minuscule amounts
8. Klutz
9. I have ___ good authority
10. *The X-Files* agent Scully
11. Hardly gregarious
19. Chain-wearing *The A-Team* actor
21. PC "oops" key
24. Battering device
25. A prospector might get a lode of it
26. ___ Tomé and Príncipe
27. Gardner of film
29. Often-hectic hosp. areas
30. Teacher's fave
31. Asner and Wynn
34. Made an attempt
37. Movie backdrop
39. *My Gal* ___

# Crossword Puzzle 20

SOLUTION PAGE 234

41. Speeder spotter
43. Winnie the ___
44. Thomas ___ Edison
46. A woodwind
47. Breathing rattle
48. One taking a gander
49. Sandwich letters

51. Bush spokesman Fleischer

## ACROSS

1. Field's yield
5. Chat room guffaw
8. Jail unit
12. Syllables from Santa
13. ___ were you...
14. Puerto ___
15. Money for the poor
16. Take one's cuts
17. Rooney of *60 Minutes*
18. Bother
20. Tide type
22. First Lady before Michelle
24. Word with gender or generation
27. Bunch of bees
31. Capital of New Mexico
33. Toy with a tail
34. Wire diameter measure
35. Actress Meg
36. Certain triathlete
38. Stadium levels
39. Energy
40. Quarrel
42. Agt.'s take
43. Fitted one within another
48. Petite or jumbo
51. Uganda's ___ Amin
53. Bees' home
54. ...with a banjo on my ___
55. Ready or ___ ...
56. I knew ___ instant...
57. Pull sharply
58. Sleet-covered
59. Confined, with "up"

## DOWN

1. I say, old ___
2. Part in a play
3. Electrical units
4. Newsgroup message
5. Follower of Virgo
6. Son-gun filler
7. Without metaphor
8. Sea creature that moves sideways
9. Ich bin ___ Berliner: JFK
10. Watch readout, briefly
11. *The Thin Man* actress Myrna
19. Stately tree
21. Blackball
23. On, as medication
24. Marvin of Motown
25. From quite a distance
26. Ink dispensers
27. Uno card
28. Barbed ___
29. Perched on
30. Stimpy's cartoon buddy
32. One less than quadri-
34. Drink with an olive
37. PC alternative
38. Summer shirt
41. Like-mindedness

**106**

# Crossword Puzzle 21

SOLUTION PAGE 235

42. Sneak preview
44. Use FedEx, say
45. Fork prong
46. Former Sen. Bayh of Indiana
47. Fender flaw
48. Where a telescope is aimed
49. Once ___ lifetime

50. Chinese discipline
52. Med school grad

## ACROSS

1. Educ. support group
4. Divan
8. Flexible, electrically
12. Japanese coin
13. Roman poet
14. Small container for liquids
15. Out of sight!
16. Mr. Uncool
17. Honolulu's island
18. Cure-all potion
20. Baltimore baseballer
22. Doorway welcomer
23. Actor Beatty
24. TV's Gomer
27. Network with annual awards
28. Dental deg.
31. ___ of Arc
32. Zodiac lion
33. Airshow stunt
34. Dine in the evening
35. Not very many
36. Lions and tigers and bears
   follower
37. Cow comment
38. Winter malady
40. All I got was this lousy ___
43. Rat or squirrel
47. Go ___ smoke
48. Hymn word
50. How about that?!
51. Lie in the sun

52. Seen once in a blue moon
53. Canine warning
54. Iowa college town
55. Easter egg decorator
56. Hither's partner

## DOWN

1. Flammable pile
2. Blue-green hue
3. *The King* ___
4. Braga of *Kiss of the Spider Woman*
5. Out-in-the-open
6. Needle producer
7. Expand, as a house
8. Keep one's distance from
9. Arrivederci
10. Roald who wrote *James and the Giant Peach*
11. Colonel Mustard's game
19. Mutant superheroes of comic books
21. Sun. speaker
24. Jammies
25. "___ Light Up My Life"
26. Once around the track
27. Kitten's sound
28. Homer Simpson outburst
29. Title for Pierre Pérignon
30. Work under cover
32. Dancer's bodysuit
33. Ear-busting

# Crossword Puzzle 22

SOLUTION PAGE 235

35. "A Bell ___ Adano"
37. Explosive devices
38. "___ Jacques" (children's song)
39. Asocial type
40. Oompah band instrument
41. Inbox junk

42. Take to the trail
44. Like an omelet
45. Roman "fiddler"
46. Bird with a forked tail
49. Memorial Day month

## ACROSS

1. Fourscore and seven years ___ ...
4. Hospital area: Abbr.
7. 180° from NNW
10. Drug cop
12. Dorm overseers, for short
13. Flippered mammal
14. Nonwinners
16. Have a chat
17. ___ Major (Big Dipper)
18. Stadium toppers
19. Grand stories
22. Pet on *The Flintstones*
24. Former *Entertainment Tonight* host
25. From Tuscany, e.g.
29. Office worker just for the day
30. The time ___ come!
31. Senate errand runner
32. Runner-up
34. "Since ___ You Baby" (1956 hit)
35. ___ of the Unknown Soldier
36. Antiquated exclamation
37. Aerosol
40. Teenage woe
42. Café au ___
43. Large sailing vessel
47. Songwriter Guthrie
48. Oft-stubbed digit
49. Scruff of the neck
50. When doubled, a nasty fly
51. Picnic intruder
52. Lobster eater's wear

## DOWN

1. I'd like to buy ___ , Pat
2. Guy's honey
3. Hospital areas: Abbr.
4. Gershwin and others
5. Pizza topping
6. Start of some aircraft carriers
7. Sewing connection
8. Clearance event
9. Antlered animals
11. Boob tube addict
13. Informer
15. $200 Monopoly properties: Abbr.
18. Crime scene evidence
19. Blues singer ___ James
20. Banana skin
21. Beliefs
23. ___ in the bag!
26. "___ Rock": Simon & Garfunkel hit
27. Grew older
28. Butterfly catchers
30. Popular Easter dish
33. Trigger's rider

# Crossword Puzzle 23

SOLUTION PAGE 235

36. Former Roxy Music member Brian
37. Venetian blind part
38. Scores to shoot for
39. Anger, with "up"
41. Atkins of country music
43. RR depot

44. Catch in the act
45. Prefix with dermis
46. Confederate soldier

## ACROSS

1. Stuff (in)
5. Ale server
8. Homecoming attender
12. Filly's father
13. 180° from WNW
14. Completely demolish
15. Look-alike
18. Window framework
19. Wire measurement
20. "___ Lang Syne"
23. Nasty looks
27. Halloween word
30. Tranquilizer gun projectile
32. Shredded side dish
33. Works
35. Agreeable response
36. Dreamcast game company
37. The "A" of IRA: Abbr.
38. Swedish car
40. Fido's doc
41. Grain bundle
43. Talking equine of TV
45. "___ Sawyer"
47. Speak highly of
50. Coin motto
56. King of Shakespeare
57. 1960s war zone, briefly
58. Chinese: Comb. form
59. Fortune's partner
60. Double-curve letter
61. Crammer's concern

## DOWN

1. CBS police series
2. Clears (of)
3. Carpeting calculation
4. High-IQ group
5. I.M. the architect
6. The Trojans of the NCAA
7. Smile from ear to ear
8. Lacking guile
9. Attorney's profession
10. Israeli arm
11. Stag party attendees
16. Dull impact sound
17. Rapper ___ Wayne
21. Puts down
22. Bedtime story?
24. Abbr. on a contour map
25. All the ___: widely popular
26. Whack
27. Arm: Fr.
28. Toe stubber's cry
29. ___ upon a time
31. Ivan the Terrible, e.g.
34. Level of achievement
39. Gamblers place them
42. Part of FYI
44. Put out, as a fire
46. Selfish one's exclamation
48. Operating system
   developed at Bell Labs
49. Bluefin, for one
50. Santa's helper

# Crossword Puzzle 24

SOLUTION PAGE 235

51. Shooter pellet
52. On the ___ : fleeing
53. Kind of relief
54. Vocal stumbles
55. Hi ___ ! (fan's message)

## ACROSS

1. Tiny branch
5. Sounds of hesitation
8. Curved path
11. Leading in the game
13. The "p" in r.p.m.
14. Cultural funding grp.
15. Midsection
16. Mas' mates
17. J–N connector
18. Scored 100 percent on
20. Runner's circuit
21. Ars gratia artis studio
24. Con's opposite
25. Country singer Ritter
26. Lawrence of ___
29. Philosopher's question
31. Coffee that won't keep you up
32. Bankrupt energy company
36. Cough medicine amt.
38. Applies, as finger paint
39. No thanks
41. Folk singer DiFranco
43. Rx watchdog
44. Grassy clump
45. Basic idea
47. Wine and dine
48. Not pro
49. Lion sounds
54. AOL or MSN: Abbr.
55. Modifying word: Abbr.
56. Popular Internet company
57. Retrieve
58. Ewe's plaint
59. Interstate exit

## DOWN

1. Work on a doily
2. Sci-fi's *Doctor* ___
3. Ending with cash or bombard
4. Tank filler
5. Like one of the two jaws
6. Pasture
7. Grads-to-be: Abbr.
8. Joint above the foot
9. Stop worrying!
10. Kid's summer spot
12. ___ double take
19. Tax preparer, for short
21. Insane
22. Test for PhD wannabes
23. Rock's Fleetwood ___
25. Daly of *Judging Amy*
27. Soaking site
28. No ___, ands, or buts
30. Skirt edge
33. Brit. flying group
34. California's Fort ___
35. Govt. code crackers
37. Chinese temple
38. Female sib
39. Condemned's neckwear?

# Crossword Puzzle 25

SOLUTION PAGE 236

40. Take in, as a stray
42. Japanese fighter
44. Big swallow
46. Hear, as a case
48. It's hailed in cities
50. Rower's need
51. Cry of discovery

52. CD-___
53. Absorb, with "up"

## ACROSS

1. Steee-rike! caller
4. Nuke
7. Govt. Rx watchdog
10. Flub
12. Made in the ___
13. Walrus relative
14. Achilles' weak spot
15. Take it on the ___
16. Salon job
17. Flightless Aussie bird
19. A long way
20. Title holder
23. Suffix with hypn-
25. Alex Haley saga
26. Let's hear more!
29. Dog command
30. Mooer
31. Palindromic cheer
33. Oklahoma native
36. Literary category
38. Guys' mates
39. Pig sounds
40. Knifelike
43. Former rival of AT&T
44. TV, slangily, with "the"
45. ___-Magnon man
47. Data, for short
51. Planets
52. Concealed
53. Like service station rags
54. Tire layer
55. Stomach muscles, briefly
56. Film producer Roach

## DOWN

1. Sound of discomfort
2. A Stooge
3. "The Fall of the House of Usher" writer
4. South African native
5. Happy ___ lark
6. Actress Dawber
7. Grope
8. Take risks
9. Donations for the poor
11. Group of ships
13. Nutmeg, e.g.
18. Bride's title
19. Cambridge sch.
20. Planet, poetically
21. Miseries
22. Like a scrubbed space mission
23. Stinks
24. Wrecker's service
27. Country music's Loretta
28. Merry escapade
30. Cartoon collectible
32. Affirmative
34. Fairy tale monsters
35. Catch forty winks
36. *You've ___ Mail*
37. Refrain in "Old MacDonald"

# Crossword Puzzle 26

SOLUTION PAGE 236

40. Go no further
41. Toss
42. Dear advice columnist
43. Mount Olympus dwellers
45. Half a dance's name
46. Adam's spare part
48. Biomedical research org.

49. It's south of Ga.
50. Animated Olive

## ACROSS

1. Roman 300
4. Oil treatment letters
7. Mail off
11. Military mail drop: Abbr.
12. Neckwear
14. *Metamorphoses* poet
15. Used a stool
16. Welder's gas
18. ___ Martin (James Bond car)
20. ___ Scotia
21. Non-Rx
22. Loewe's partner on Broadway
26. Comics orphan
28. Director Craven
29. "Evil Woman" band
30. Mediterranean fruits
19. Football Hall of Famer Dawson
32. Carpenter's fastener
33. Folk rocker DiFranco
34. Sch. near Harvard
35. In base eight
36. Alamo offering
38. Brit. fliers
39. Periods in history
41. Waterproof covers
44. "Jimmy Crack Corn" sentiment
48. Ich bin ___ Berliner
49. Lumberjacks' tools
50. Hit with the fist
51. Storekeeper on *The Simpsons*
52. Gomer of TV
53. Alternative to coffee
54. Beer barrel

## DOWN

1. Spanish house
2. Tax pros: Abbr.
3. Eli Whitney invention
4. Batter's position
5. Quirky habit
6. Hammerhead part
7. Renewable energy type
8. New Year's ___
9. *Collages* author Anaïs
10. Ike's monogram
13. Ripped off
17. Designer Saint Laurent
19. Soul singer Redding
23. Compulsive cleaner
24. Film director Kazan
25. Bread basket choice
26. It's ___ cry from...
27. Cloud number
28. More than damp
31. Purple flowers
32. Final Four inits.
34. "Who Needs the Kwik-E-___?" (song from *The Simpsons*)
35. Sandinista leader Daniel

# Crossword Puzzle 27

SOLUTION PAGE 236

37. All wound up
40. Shaker contents
42. Sherlock Holmes item
43. Skintight
44. AOL or EarthLink, for example: Abbr.
45. *The ___ of the Jackal*

46. Wise bird
47. Feel regret over

## ACROSS

1. Tanning lotion letters
4. Uncertainties
7. Hell of a guy?
12. Mauna ___
13. Medical research agcy.
14. Share one's views
15. News-service letters
16. Arid
17. Place to do the hustle
18. Parisian thanks
20. Gather, as information
21. Mus. majors' degrees
23. Corporate VIP
24. Yeses at sea
27. Love ___ neighbor...
29. ___ bladder
33. Bear lair
34. ___ room: play area
35. Orchestra area
36. Coffee, slangily
38. Hole punching tool
39. Potato
40. Phoenix-to-Seattle dir.
42. Cry of fear
44. Kemo Sabe's companion
47. Far-reaching view
51. Bikini Island, e.g.
52. Tournament exemption
54. No. on a business card
55. Stanford ___ test
56. ___ voyage!
57. Egyptian reptile
58. Movie music
59. Paste's partner
60. Classic muscle car

## DOWN

1. Blighted urban area
2. Vatican leader
3. Light-skinned
4. Calcutta's home
5. Balsam, e.g.
6. A little short, as of money
7. Manage to avoid
8. Novel postscript
9. Clamp
10. Machu Picchu builder
11. Explorer Ponce de ___
19. *60 Minutes* network
22. Stable bedding
23. Go by bike
24. Dictionary abbreviation
25. Nay opposer
26. Ltr. holder
28. Chop
30. Killer computer program
31. Brooklyn campus: Abbr.
32. Inc., in England
37. Buck's defense
39. Go down a slippery slope
41. *The Prince of Tides* star Nick
43. Episode
44. Keep ___ on (watch)

# Crossword Puzzle 28

SOLUTION PAGE 236

45. Hearing-related

46. Faux pas

48. Fawn's father

49. Final or midterm

50. Brand for Fido

52. UK TV network

53. Golden Rule pronoun

## ACROSS

1. Affectionate embraces
5. Tabloid fliers
9. Mustache site
12. Words before uproar or instant
13. Snare
14. Zsa Zsa's sister
15. Card game for one
17. Floor covering
18. Obviously!
19. Carbon copy
21. Sticky problem
24. Welles or Bean
26. Provide weapons for
27. Just dandy
29. ___ Romeo: sports car
32. Like some tea
34. Last letter
35. Seriously injure
36. Over hill and ___
37. Acorn producers
39. Dryly humorous
40. Tennis great Ivan
42. Sniffers
44. Arcade game maker
46. What golfers try to break
47. Prickly husk
48. Kitchen gadget that turns
54. Paleozoic, for one
55. Barely earned, with "out"
56. Do as directed
57. Blasting stuff
58. Pied Piper followers
59. Drink with unagi

## DOWN

1. ___ and hers
2. Numero ___
3. *My ___ Sal*
4. Nasty, as a remark
5. 2002 Winter Olympics locale
6. TGIF day
7. Boat mover
8. Glasses, informally
9. Car buyers' protection
10. As a czar, he was terrible
11. Chopped liver spread
16. Surf and ___
20. Good farm soil
21. Picked up the tab
22. Willy of *Free Willy*
23. Suspect dishonesty
24. Ryan of *Love Story*
25. Smell strongly
28. Polo Ralph Lauren competitor
30. Cannoneer's command
31. Writers Lowell and Tan
33. Bambi's kin
38. Attention-getting sound
41. More friendly
43. Nabisco cookies
44. Aid and ___

# Crossword Puzzle 29

SOLUTION PAGE 237

45. Chance to play in a game
46. Pea holders
49. Alias letters
50. Butterfly catcher's tool
51. Wizards and Magic org.
52. Mouse sighter's cry
53. Bread with seeds

## ACROSS

1. Prefix with morphosis
5. Univ., e.g.
8. Former Florida governor Bush
11. Make, as money
12. Election day, e.g.: Abbr.
13. "___ Lama Ding Dong"
14. Sandpaper coating
15. Sleep phenomenon: Abbr.
16. Enthusiastic
17. Lacking pigment
19. Take to the sky
21. Part of a semi
22. Diva Merriman
23. NASCAR measure
26. *Charlotte's* ___
28. Socially challenged
32. Regard as
34. ___-boom-bah
36. Truth or ___ (slumber party game)
37. Jack of nursery rhyme
39. Gift adornment
41. Recipe amt.
42. Stewart or Steiger
44. PC linkup
46. Masthead title
49. Starting point
53. HS subject
54. PC maker
56. ___ bene
57. ___ Minor (constellation)
58. August 1 sign
59. *Iliad* setting
60. The limit, proverbially
61. Football great Dawson
62. Nest egg protectors?

## DOWN

1. ___ Millions (lottery)
2. British nobleman
3. Chicago paper, briefly
4. Playful trick
5. Disco lights
6. Pool stick
7. Charles Atlas, for one
8. Coffee, in slang
9. Give off, as light
10. Florida's Miami- ___ County
13. ___ out (postponed, in a way)
18. No, slangily
20. Moving truck
23. Physicians: Abbr.
24. ___ pill (amphetamine)
25. *How Stella Got ___ Groove Back*
27. Baby's neckwear
29. Urban vermin
30. ER workers
31. Cowboy's assent
33. Mrs. Washington
35. Wise king of Israel

# Crossword Puzzle 30

SOLUTION PAGE 237

38. This ___ shall pass
40. Armed conflict
43. Dentist's tool
45. Final inning, usually
46. Aussie birds
47. Like the night
48. Teensy

50. Al or Tipper
51. Lay ___ the line
52. Anti votes
55. Honey maker

# Sudoku Puzzles

## Sudoku Puzzle 1

| | 2 | | | | | | 3 | |
|---|---|---|---|---|---|---|---|---|
| | | | | | | 4 | | 9 |
| 1 | 6 | 9 | | 8 | 3 | 2 | | |
| | 8 | | | 9 | | 3 | | 4 |
| | 4 | 3 | | | | 6 | 7 | |
| 7 | | 5 | | 3 | | | 8 | |
| | | 6 | 3 | 7 | | 1 | 2 | 8 |
| 8 | | 1 | | | | | | |
| | 9 | | | | | | 4 | |

SOLUTION PAGE 238

## Sudoku Puzzle 2

| 9 |   |   | 4 |   | 6 |   |   | 7 |
|---|---|---|---|---|---|---|---|---|
| 2 | 4 |   |   |   |   |   | 6 | 9 |
|   |   | 7 | 9 |   | 2 | 4 |   |   |
| 1 |   |   | 6 |   | 3 |   |   | 2 |
|   |   |   |   |   |   |   |   |   |
| 7 |   |   | 1 |   | 5 |   |   | 4 |
|   |   | 9 | 5 |   | 1 | 8 |   |   |
| 3 | 2 |   |   |   |   |   | 7 | 5 |
| 8 |   |   | 7 |   | 9 |   |   | 6 |

SOLUTION PAGE 238

# Sudoku Puzzle 3

| 4 | 9 |   |   | 1 | 6 | 7 |   |   |
|---|---|---|---|---|---|---|---|---|
|   | 7 |   |   | 8 |   |   |   |   |
|   |   |   | 7 |   |   | 1 | 4 |   |
| 6 | 4 |   |   | 3 |   |   |   | 5 |
| 7 | 1 |   |   |   |   |   | 9 | 6 |
| 5 |   |   |   | 7 |   |   | 3 | 1 |
|   | 5 | 4 |   |   | 9 |   |   |   |
|   |   |   |   | 4 |   |   | 8 |   |
|   |   | 7 | 8 | 5 |   |   | 6 | 4 |

SOLUTION PAGE 238

## Sudoku Puzzle 4

| | 9 | | 1 | | | | | |
| 5 | | 3 | 9 | | | | 1 |
| | | 4 | | 8 | 5 | | 2 |
| 9 | | 2 | | | | 8 | 4 | |
| | 1 | | 2 | | 9 | | |
| | 8 | 5 | | | | 2 | | 3 |
| 8 | | 6 | 7 | | 1 | | | |
| 1 | | | 8 | 6 | | 5 | |
| | | | | 4 | | 6 | |

SOLUTION PAGE 238

## Sudoku Puzzle 5

| | 6 | | 2 | | 8 | | 5 | |
|---|---|---|---|---|---|---|---|---|
| | | 8 | | | | 9 | | |
| 3 | | 5 | 7 | | 1 | 6 | | 8 |
| 6 | 3 | | 9 | | 2 | | 4 | 7 |
| | | | | | | | | |
| 4 | 7 | | 5 | | 3 | | 8 | 9 |
| 1 | | 3 | 4 | | 7 | 2 | | 6 |
| | | 6 | | | | 7 | | |
| | 9 | | 3 | | 6 | | 1 | |

SOLUTION PAGE 239

# Sudoku Puzzle 6

| 4 | 5 | 7 | 1 | 9 |   |   |   |   |
|---|---|---|---|---|---|---|---|---|
| 1 |   |   |   |   |   |   | 6 |   |
|   |   |   |   |   | 2 |   |   | 5 |
| 5 | 7 |   | 4 |   | 9 |   | 2 |   |
|   | 2 |   |   | 1 |   |   | 4 |   |
|   | 9 |   | 2 |   | 3 |   | 8 | 1 |
| 2 |   |   | 3 |   |   |   |   |   |
|   | 3 |   |   |   |   |   |   | 8 |
|   |   |   |   | 7 | 1 | 2 | 9 | 3 |

SOLUTION PAGE 239

131

## Sudoku Puzzle 7

| 8 |   | 7 |   | 3 |   |   |   |   |
|---|---|---|---|---|---|---|---|---|
|   |   | 2 | 1 | 4 |   |   |   | 9 |
| 4 | 1 |   | 2 |   |   |   |   |   |
| 5 |   |   |   |   | 3 | 9 |   | 1 |
|   | 2 |   |   | 8 |   |   | 6 |   |
| 9 |   | 8 | 6 |   |   |   |   | 4 |
|   |   |   |   |   | 7 |   | 4 | 3 |
| 1 |   |   | 5 | 2 | 6 |   |   |   |
|   |   |   | 6 |   | 2 |   |   | 8 |

SOLUTION PAGE 239

## Sudoku Puzzle 8

|   |   | 7 | 1 | 3 | 4 |   | 2 | 5 |
|---|---|---|---|---|---|---|---|---|
|   |   |   | 7 | 2 |   |   |   |   |
|   |   |   |   |   | 6 |   | 4 |   |
| 6 | 7 | 3 |   | 1 |   |   |   | 9 |
| 9 |   |   |   |   |   |   |   | 6 |
| 1 |   |   |   | 6 |   | 3 | 7 | 4 |
|   | 6 |   | 8 |   |   |   |   |   |
|   |   |   |   | 4 | 5 |   |   |   |
| 4 | 3 |   | 2 | 7 | 1 | 9 |   |   |

SOLUTION PAGE 239

## Sudoku Puzzle 9

| 8 | 9 |   | 6 |   | 2 |   | 1 | 3 |
|---|---|---|---|---|---|---|---|---|
| 3 |   |   | 1 |   | 8 |   |   | 5 |
|   |   |   |   |   |   |   |   |   |
|   | 3 | 4 | 9 |   | 5 | 7 | 2 |   |
|   |   |   |   |   |   |   |   |   |
|   | 8 | 5 | 4 |   | 7 | 6 | 3 |   |
|   |   |   |   |   |   |   |   |   |
| 9 |   |   | 5 |   | 6 |   |   | 7 |
| 1 | 2 |   | 3 |   | 4 |   | 9 | 6 |

SOLUTION PAGE 240

## Sudoku Puzzle 10

| | | 8 | | | | 3 | 5 | |
|---|---|---|---|---|---|---|---|---|
| | | 4 | | 6 | | | | 9 |
| | 9 | | 4 | | | | 6 | |
| | | 7 | | 4 | | | 3 | 2 |
| 9 | | 3 | | 2 | | 1 | | 7 |
| 2 | 8 | | | 1 | | 9 | | |
| | 7 | | | | 3 | | 9 | |
| 3 | | | | 7 | | 2 | | |
| | 6 | 2 | | | | 5 | | |

SOLUTION PAGE 240

## Sudoku Puzzle 11

| 9 | 6 | 2 | 4 |   | 3 |   |   | 5 |
|---|---|---|---|---|---|---|---|---|
|   |   |   |   |   | 6 | 4 |   |   |
| 3 | 1 |   |   |   |   |   |   |   |
|   |   |   |   |   | 5 | 3 | 2 | 6 |
| 6 |   |   |   | 2 |   |   |   | 1 |
| 4 | 2 | 9 | 3 |   |   |   |   |   |
|   |   |   |   |   |   |   | 8 | 7 |
|   |   | 8 | 5 |   |   |   |   |   |
| 2 |   |   | 6 |   | 8 | 5 | 3 | 4 |

SOLUTION PAGE 240

## Sudoku Puzzle 12

| | | | 3 | 2 | | | | |
|---|---|---|---|---|---|---|---|---|
| 6 | 1 | 7 | 5 | | | 3 | | |
| | | | | | 6 | 4 | | 9 |
| 9 | 6 | | | | 1 | 2 | | |
| 1 | | | | 4 | | | | 5 |
| | | 5 | 2 | | | | 9 | 1 |
| 3 | | 1 | 4 | | | | | |
| | | 6 | | | 3 | 9 | 4 | 7 |
| | | | | 6 | 5 | | | |

SOLUTION PAGE 240

# Sudoku Puzzle 13

| | 7 | 8 | | 9 | | 3 | 5 | 1 |
|---|---|---|---|---|---|---|---|---|
| | | 5 | | | | | | |
| 1 | 2 | | | | | | | |
| 2 | | | 9 | 1 | | | 3 | |
| | 5 | | 6 | 2 | 8 | | 7 | |
| | 6 | | | 7 | 5 | | | 4 |
| | | | | | | | 9 | 5 |
| | | | | | | 6 | | |
| 5 | 9 | 3 | | 4 | | 2 | 8 | |

SOLUTION PAGE 241

# Sudoku Puzzle 14

| 4 |   | 1 |   | 8 |   | 6 |   |   |
|---|---|---|---|---|---|---|---|---|
| 5 |   |   | 9 | 2 |   |   |   | 8 |
|   | 8 | 2 |   | 3 |   | 1 |   |   |
| 3 | 6 |   |   |   |   | 7 |   |   |
| 2 |   |   |   |   |   |   |   | 4 |
|   |   | 5 |   |   |   |   | 1 | 6 |
|   |   | 9 |   | 6 |   | 3 | 4 |   |
| 8 |   |   |   | 1 | 7 |   |   | 9 |
|   |   | 3 |   | 9 |   | 5 |   | 1 |

SOLUTION PAGE 241

# Sudoku Puzzle 15

| 3 |   |   | 5 |   | 9 |   |   | 2 |
|---|---|---|---|---|---|---|---|---|
| 5 | 2 |   |   |   |   |   | 6 | 9 |
| 4 |   |   | 7 |   | 1 |   |   | 8 |
| 9 |   | 6 | 4 |   | 8 | 3 |   | 5 |
|   |   |   |   |   |   |   |   |   |
| 7 |   | 4 | 6 |   | 2 | 9 |   | 1 |
| 6 |   |   | 2 |   | 7 |   |   | 3 |
| 1 | 9 |   |   |   |   |   | 7 | 4 |
| 8 |   |   | 9 |   | 3 |   |   | 6 |

SOLUTION PAGE 241

140

# Sudoku Puzzle 16

| 1 | 5 |   | 9 |   | 7 |   | 6 | 8 |
|---|---|---|---|---|---|---|---|---|
| 3 |   |   |   |   |   |   |   | 5 |
| 8 |   | 7 |   |   |   | 2 |   | 4 |
| 4 |   |   | 1 |   | 5 |   |   | 3 |
|   |   |   |   |   |   |   |   |   |
| 6 |   |   | 3 |   | 2 |   |   | 1 |
| 5 |   | 4 |   |   |   | 8 |   | 6 |
| 7 |   |   |   |   |   |   |   | 2 |
| 2 | 8 |   | 6 |   | 4 |   | 5 | 9 |

SOLUTION PAGE 241

## Sudoku Puzzle 17

| | | 3 | 7 | | 5 | 4 | | |
|---|---|---|---|---|---|---|---|---|
| | 5 | | 2 | | 4 | | 9 | |
| 8 | 2 | | | | | | 6 | 5 |
| 5 | 4 | 8 | | | | 1 | 7 | 9 |
| | | | | | | | | |
| 2 | 3 | 6 | | | | 5 | 8 | 4 |
| 4 | 7 | | | | | | 1 | 3 |
| | 9 | | 4 | | 2 | | 5 | |
| | | 5 | 1 | | 6 | 9 | | |

SOLUTION PAGE 242

## Sudoku Puzzle 18

| 1 |   |   | 8 |   | 6 |   |   | 4 |
|---|---|---|---|---|---|---|---|---|
|   | 7 |   | 2 |   | 9 |   | 6 |   |
| 8 |   | 3 |   |   |   | 5 |   | 2 |
| 5 |   |   | 3 |   | 1 |   |   | 6 |
|   |   |   |   |   |   |   |   |   |
| 9 |   |   | 4 |   | 5 |   |   | 7 |
| 6 |   | 1 |   |   |   | 7 |   | 8 |
|   | 4 |   | 9 |   | 2 |   | 1 |   |
| 2 |   |   | 1 |   | 7 |   |   | 9 |

SOLUTION PAGE 242

# Sudoku Puzzle 19

| | 5 | 3 | | | | 2 | 9 | |
|---|---|---|---|---|---|---|---|---|
| 6 | | | 1 | | 9 | | | 5 |
| 9 | 4 | | | | | | 3 | 1 |
| | 6 | | 9 | | 5 | | 2 | |
| | | | | | | | | |
| | 2 | | 4 | | 3 | | 1 | |
| 2 | 9 | | | | | | 5 | 8 |
| 7 | | | 2 | | 8 | | | 6 |
| | 8 | 5 | | | | 3 | 7 | |

SOLUTION PAGE 242

## Sudoku Puzzle 20

| 4 | 1 |   | 7 |   |   |   |   |   |
|---|---|---|---|---|---|---|---|---|
|   |   |   |   |   |   |   | 1 |   |
| 5 | 6 | 9 |   | 3 |   | 4 |   |   |
|   | 9 | 6 | 1 | 7 |   |   |   | 4 |
|   |   | 2 |   | 6 |   | 7 |   |   |
| 7 |   |   |   | 8 | 3 | 6 | 2 |   |
|   |   | 4 |   | 9 |   | 1 | 6 | 3 |
|   | 5 |   |   |   |   |   |   |   |
|   |   |   |   |   | 4 |   | 5 | 2 |

SOLUTION PAGE 242

# Sudoku Puzzle 21

|   |   |   |   |   |   |   |   |   |
|---|---|---|---|---|---|---|---|---|
|   |   |   |   |   |   |   |   |   |
|   | 8 | 7 | 1 |   | 4 | 3 | 6 |   |
| 6 |   | 9 |   |   |   | 5 |   | 4 |
| 9 |   | 6 | 4 |   | 2 | 1 |   | 7 |
|   |   |   |   | 1 |   |   |   |   |
| 8 |   | 2 | 5 |   | 9 | 4 |   | 6 |
| 4 |   | 3 |   |   |   | 9 |   | 1 |
|   | 6 | 1 | 3 |   | 7 | 8 | 4 |   |
|   |   |   |   |   |   |   |   |   |

SOLUTION PAGE 243

# Sudoku Puzzle 22

| | 2 | | | | | | 9 | |
|---|---|---|---|---|---|---|---|---|
| | 6 | 1 | 3 | | | | 2 | 4 |
| 5 | | 7 | 4 | | | | | 3 |
| | | 4 | | | | | | 7 |
| 7 | 3 | | | 1 | | | 5 | 2 |
| 1 | | | | | | 8 | | |
| 2 | | | | | 1 | 3 | | 9 |
| 3 | 1 | | | | 7 | 2 | 4 | |
| | 7 | | | | | | 6 | |

SOLUTION PAGE 243

# Sudoku Puzzle 23

| 5 | 3 |   | 8 |   | 2 |   | 6 | 9 |
|---|---|---|---|---|---|---|---|---|
| 6 |   |   |   |   |   |   |   | 7 |
|   |   | 7 | 6 |   | 5 | 8 |   |   |
|   |   | 6 | 3 |   | 1 | 9 |   |   |
|   |   |   |   |   |   |   |   |   |
|   |   | 2 | 7 |   | 9 | 3 |   |   |
|   |   | 8 | 2 |   | 7 | 4 |   |   |
| 2 |   |   |   |   |   |   |   | 1 |
| 4 | 9 |   | 5 |   | 3 |   | 8 | 2 |

SOLUTION PAGE 243

## Sudoku Puzzle 24

| 8 |   |   |   |   | 6 |   |   |   |
|---|---|---|---|---|---|---|---|---|
| 5 |   | 7 | 2 |   |   |   |   | 3 |
| 9 | 2 |   |   | 5 |   |   | 6 |   |
| 4 |   |   | 5 |   |   | 3 |   | 6 |
|   |   | 2 |   | 1 |   | 9 |   |   |
| 6 |   | 9 |   |   | 3 |   |   | 2 |
|   | 8 |   |   | 9 |   |   | 5 | 7 |
| 2 |   |   |   |   | 5 | 8 |   | 9 |
|   |   |   | 8 |   |   |   |   | 4 |

SOLUTION PAGE 243

# Sudoku Puzzle 25

| 8 |   |   |   |   |   |   | 4 | 7 |   |
|---|---|---|---|---|---|---|---|---|---|
| 5 |   |   | 9 | 7 | 8 | 3 |   |   |   |
|   | 9 |   |   |   |   |   |   | 8 |   |
| 4 | 5 | 6 |   |   | 2 |   |   | 7 |   |
|   |   |   |   |   |   |   |   |   |   |
| 7 |   |   | 5 |   |   | 1 | 4 | 6 |   |
| 6 |   |   |   |   |   |   | 1 |   |   |
|   |   | 5 | 2 | 1 | 7 |   |   | 4 |   |
|   | 4 | 8 |   |   |   |   |   | 2 |   |

SOLUTION PAGE 244

# Sudoku Puzzle 26

| 6 |   | 5 | 3 |   | 8 | 7 |   | 2 |
|---|---|---|---|---|---|---|---|---|
|   |   |   |   |   |   |   |   |   |
| 1 |   | 2 |   |   |   | 8 |   | 9 |
| 2 | 4 |   | 9 |   | 1 |   | 5 | 3 |
|   |   |   |   |   |   |   |   |   |
| 3 | 5 |   | 6 |   | 7 |   | 8 | 4 |
| 5 |   | 4 |   |   |   | 3 |   | 8 |
|   |   |   |   |   |   |   |   |   |
| 7 |   | 1 | 4 |   | 6 | 9 |   | 5 |

SOLUTION PAGE 244

# Sudoku Puzzle 27

| 9 | 1 | 7 |   |   | 3 | 5 | 2 |   |
|---|---|---|---|---|---|---|---|---|
| 5 |   |   |   | 1 |   | 3 |   |   |
|   |   |   |   |   | 7 |   | 9 | 8 |
| 3 |   |   |   |   |   | 6 |   |   |
| 1 |   |   |   | 5 |   |   |   | 9 |
|   |   | 2 |   |   |   |   |   | 1 |
| 7 | 3 |   | 6 |   |   |   |   |   |
|   |   | 8 |   | 2 |   |   |   | 6 |
|   | 6 | 1 | 7 |   |   | 8 | 5 | 3 |

SOLUTION PAGE 244

## Sudoku Puzzle 28

| | 9 | 1 | | | 3 | | 4 | |
| 4 | | | 8 | | 9 | | | 3 |
| 3 | | 5 | | 6 | | | 7 | |
| | 7 | | | | | | | |
| 1 | | | 7 | 8 | 6 | | | 5 |
| | | | | | | | 6 | |
| | 1 | | | 3 | | 5 | | 2 |
| 6 | | | 5 | | 8 | | | 4 |
| | 5 | | 9 | | | 3 | 8 | |

SOLUTION PAGE 244

## Sudoku Puzzle 29

| | | 2 | 4 | 9 | 5 | | 1 | |
|---|---|---|---|---|---|---|---|---|
| 8 | | | | 6 | | | | 2 |
| | | | | | | | | |
| 2 | | | 1 | 5 | | 6 | | 3 |
| 6 | | 3 | | | | 2 | | 8 |
| 4 | | 8 | | 2 | 6 | | | 9 |
| | | | | | | | | |
| 1 | | | | 4 | | | | 6 |
| | 3 | | 2 | 1 | 7 | 9 | | |

SOLUTION PAGE 245

# Sudoku Puzzle 30

| 5 |   | 7 | 9 |   | 1 | 3 |   | 8 |
|---|---|---|---|---|---|---|---|---|
| 9 | 8 |   |   |   |   |   | 2 | 5 |
|   |   |   | 5 |   | 4 |   |   |   |
| 8 | 5 |   | 1 |   | 6 |   | 3 | 2 |
|   |   |   |   |   |   |   |   |   |
| 4 | 3 |   | 8 |   | 7 |   | 5 | 1 |
|   |   |   | 4 |   | 2 |   |   |   |
| 2 | 6 |   |   |   |   |   | 4 | 7 |
| 1 |   | 4 | 6 |   | 9 | 2 |   | 3 |

SOLUTION PAGE 245

# Sudoku Puzzle 31

| 7 |   | 5 | 6 |   | 8 | 9 |   | 2 |
|---|---|---|---|---|---|---|---|---|
| 8 |   |   | 4 |   | 5 |   |   | 6 |
|   |   |   |   |   |   |   |   |   |
| 9 | 8 |   | 1 |   | 4 |   | 2 | 7 |
|   |   |   |   |   |   |   |   |   |
| 3 | 5 |   | 9 |   | 7 |   | 8 | 1 |
|   |   |   |   |   |   |   |   |   |
| 4 |   |   | 2 |   | 6 |   |   | 3 |
| 2 |   | 9 | 5 |   | 1 | 6 |   | 8 |

SOLUTION PAGE 245

156

# Sudoku Puzzle 32

| | 7 | 5 | 3 | | | 4 | | 2 |
|---|---|---|---|---|---|---|---|---|
| 6 | 3 | | | | 5 | | 8 | 1 |
| 4 | | 2 | | | | | | |
| | | | | | | | | 4 |
| 9 | | | 8 | | 7 | | | 3 |
| 1 | | | | | | | | |
| | | | | | | 2 | | 7 |
| 7 | 9 | | 2 | | | | 4 | 8 |
| 2 | | 4 | | | 6 | 5 | 1 | |

SOLUTION PAGE 245

## Sudoku Puzzle 33

| | 6 | | | 8 | | 9 | | |
|---|---|---|---|---|---|---|---|---|
| 5 | 3 | | | 4 | | | | 6 |
| | | | | | | 7 | 5 | |
| | 9 | | 6 | | | | | 3 |
| 8 | 5 | | 7 | 1 | 4 | | 6 | 9 |
| 1 | | | | | 3 | | 7 | |
| | 1 | 4 | | | | | | |
| 6 | | | | 5 | | | 4 | 7 |
| | | 5 | | 3 | | | 9 | |

SOLUTION PAGE 246

# Sudoku Puzzle 34

| 5 |   | 1 | 2 | 3 | 7 |   |   |   |
|---|---|---|---|---|---|---|---|---|
|   |   | 8 |   |   |   | 1 |   |   |
|   | 2 | 6 |   |   |   |   |   | 5 |
|   |   | 5 |   | 2 |   |   | 6 |   |
| 1 |   | 7 |   | 5 |   | 2 |   | 4 |
|   | 8 |   |   | 4 |   | 5 |   |   |
| 6 |   |   |   |   |   | 7 | 1 |   |
|   |   | 9 |   |   |   | 6 |   |   |
|   |   |   | 1 | 6 | 5 | 9 |   | 3 |

SOLUTION PAGE 246

# Sudoku Puzzle 35

| 1 |   | 8 | 6 | 7 |   | 5 |   |   |
|---|---|---|---|---|---|---|---|---|
|   |   |   |   |   |   |   | 8 |   |
| 6 |   |   | 5 | 8 | 1 |   |   |   |
| 9 |   |   |   | 5 | 8 |   | 6 | 2 |
| 2 |   |   |   |   |   |   |   | 4 |
| 5 | 3 |   | 9 | 6 |   |   |   | 1 |
|   |   |   | 8 | 1 | 5 |   |   | 7 |
|   | 5 |   |   |   |   |   |   |   |
|   |   | 1 |   | 9 | 4 | 2 |   | 5 |

SOLUTION PAGE 246

# Sudoku Puzzle 36

| 1 |   | 9 |   | 7 |   |   |   |   |
|---|---|---|---|---|---|---|---|---|
|   |   | 8 | 9 |   |   |   | 3 | 5 |
|   |   |   | 6 |   |   | 9 |   |   |
|   | 8 |   |   |   | 1 |   |   | 2 |
|   | 9 | 5 |   |   |   | 8 | 1 |   |
| 6 |   |   | 4 |   |   |   | 5 |   |
|   |   | 4 |   |   | 6 |   |   |   |
| 8 | 5 |   |   |   | 9 | 4 |   |   |
|   |   |   |   | 5 |   | 1 |   | 7 |

SOLUTION PAGE 246

# Sudoku Puzzle 37

| 1 | 6 |   |   | 5 | 4 |   |   |   |
|---|---|---|---|---|---|---|---|---|
| 5 | 3 |   |   |   |   |   |   | 1 |
|   |   | 8 | 1 | 9 |   |   |   |   |
|   | 2 |   | 4 | 7 |   | 1 | 9 |   |
|   |   |   |   |   |   |   |   |   |
|   | 5 | 4 |   | 3 | 1 |   | 8 |   |
|   |   |   |   | 8 | 5 | 6 |   |   |
| 3 |   |   |   |   |   |   | 5 | 8 |
|   |   |   | 3 | 1 |   |   | 7 | 9 |

SOLUTION PAGE 247

# Sudoku Puzzle 38

| 9 | 2 |   | 7 |   | 4 |   | 5 | 3 |
|---|---|---|---|---|---|---|---|---|
|   |   |   |   |   |   |   | 4 |   |
| 5 | 4 |   |   |   |   |   | 7 | 6 |
|   | 6 |   | 9 | 5 |   |   |   |   |
|   |   |   | 3 | 1 | 7 |   |   |   |
|   |   |   |   | 6 | 2 |   | 9 |   |
| 4 | 3 |   |   |   |   |   | 2 | 5 |
|   | 7 |   |   |   |   |   |   |   |
| 1 | 5 |   | 8 |   | 3 |   | 6 | 9 |

SOLUTION PAGE 247

## Sudoku Puzzle 39

| 4 | 8 |   | 5 |   | 3 |   | 7 | 2 |
|---|---|---|---|---|---|---|---|---|
| 5 |   |   |   |   |   |   |   |   |
|   |   | 9 | 7 |   |   | 8 |   |   |
|   |   | 3 |   |   | 6 |   |   | 8 |
| 2 |   |   |   |   |   |   |   | 9 |
| 1 |   |   | 8 |   |   | 4 |   |   |
|   |   | 7 |   |   | 8 | 6 |   |   |
|   |   |   |   |   |   |   |   | 1 |
| 8 | 5 |   | 6 |   | 9 |   | 4 | 7 |

SOLUTION PAGE 247

164

# Sudoku Puzzle 40

| 6 |   |   |   | 1 |   |   | 9 | 4 |
|---|---|---|---|---|---|---|---|---|
| 1 |   | 9 | 5 |   |   | 6 |   |   |
|   |   |   |   |   | 9 |   |   | 1 |
| 8 |   |   |   | 3 | 7 |   |   |   |
|   |   | 3 |   |   |   | 9 |   |   |
|   |   |   | 9 | 5 |   |   |   | 6 |
| 5 |   |   | 6 |   |   |   |   |   |
|   |   | 4 |   |   | 8 | 2 |   | 5 |
| 3 | 8 |   |   | 4 |   |   |   | 9 |

SOLUTION PAGE 247

# Sudoku Puzzle 41

| 6 | 2 |   | 8 | 3 |   | 1 |   |   |
|---|---|---|---|---|---|---|---|---|
|   | 4 | 8 | 2 |   | 1 |   | 3 |   |
| 9 |   |   |   |   |   |   | 6 |   |
| 4 |   |   | 3 |   |   |   |   |   |
|   | 7 |   |   |   |   |   | 8 |   |
|   |   |   |   |   | 7 |   |   | 5 |
|   | 8 |   |   |   |   |   |   | 6 |
|   | 5 |   | 6 |   | 8 | 7 | 9 |   |
|   |   | 4 |   | 9 | 3 |   | 1 | 8 |

SOLUTION PAGE 248

# Sudoku Puzzle 42

|   |   |   |   | 4 | 8 | 5 | 2 |   |
|---|---|---|---|---|---|---|---|---|
| 4 | 5 |   |   |   |   |   |   | 6 |
|   |   |   | 5 |   |   | 8 |   | 1 |
| 8 |   | 1 |   |   | 5 | 2 |   |   |
|   |   |   |   | 3 |   |   |   |   |
|   |   | 6 | 2 |   |   | 4 |   | 8 |
| 5 |   | 7 |   |   | 1 |   |   |   |
|   | 6 |   |   |   |   |   | 1 | 5 |
|   | 1 | 4 | 7 | 5 |   |   |   |   |

SOLUTION PAGE 248

## Sudoku Puzzle 43

| | | 3 | | 9 | | 2 | | |
|---|---|---|---|---|---|---|---|---|
| 5 | | | | 1 | 6 | | | |
| 7 | 2 | | | | 8 | | | |
| 2 | | | | | | 6 | 7 | |
| 8 | | | 6 | | 1 | | | 9 |
| | 3 | 6 | | | | | | 4 |
| | | | 5 | | | | 3 | 7 |
| | | | 8 | 3 | | | | 5 |
| | | 5 | | 6 | | 9 | | |

SOLUTION PAGE 248

## Sudoku Puzzle 44

| 5 |   |   | 3 | 2 | 7 |   |   |   |
|---|---|---|---|---|---|---|---|---|
| 7 | 2 |   |   | 5 |   |   |   |   |
|   |   | 3 | 1 |   | 8 |   |   |   |
|   | 3 | 4 |   |   |   |   | 2 | 5 |
| 1 | 5 |   |   |   |   |   | 6 | 3 |
| 2 | 6 |   |   |   |   | 1 | 8 |   |
|   |   |   | 9 |   | 5 | 4 |   |   |
|   |   |   |   | 6 |   |   | 1 | 9 |
|   |   |   | 2 | 7 | 1 |   |   | 6 |

SOLUTION PAGE 248

## Sudoku Puzzle 45

| 3 | 6 | 1 |   |   | 8 |   |   |   |
|---|---|---|---|---|---|---|---|---|
| 7 |   |   |   |   |   |   |   |   |
| 2 | 8 |   |   |   | 9 |   | 1 |   |
| 6 |   |   | 9 |   | 7 |   |   | 3 |
| 1 | 5 |   | 6 |   | 4 |   | 9 | 7 |
| 9 |   |   | 5 |   | 1 |   |   | 4 |
|   | 9 |   | 4 |   |   |   | 6 | 1 |
|   |   |   |   |   |   |   |   | 2 |
|   |   |   | 8 |   |   | 5 | 7 | 9 |

SOLUTION PAGE 249

# Sudoku Puzzle 46

| 5 | 2 | 1 | 9 |   |   |   |   |   |
|---|---|---|---|---|---|---|---|---|
|   |   | 3 |   | 4 |   |   |   |   |
|   |   |   | 3 |   |   |   | 9 | 5 |
| 4 |   | 7 |   |   |   |   | 6 |   |
| 2 |   |   | 8 | 1 | 6 |   |   | 7 |
|   | 8 |   |   |   |   | 1 |   | 3 |
| 7 | 4 |   |   |   | 3 |   |   |   |
|   |   |   |   | 5 |   | 2 |   |   |
|   |   |   |   |   | 4 | 3 | 7 | 6 |

SOLUTION PAGE 249

## Sudoku Puzzle 47

| 5 | 9 | 3 | 8 |   |   |   |   |   |
|---|---|---|---|---|---|---|---|---|
| 2 | 6 |   | 7 |   |   |   |   |   |
|   |   |   |   | 9 |   |   |   | 2 |
| 9 |   |   |   |   | 1 | 7 |   | 8 |
|   |   | 5 |   | 6 |   | 2 |   |   |
| 8 |   | 1 | 9 |   |   |   |   | 5 |
| 6 |   |   |   | 5 |   |   |   |   |
|   |   |   |   |   | 3 |   | 2 | 4 |
|   |   |   |   |   | 7 | 9 | 1 | 6 |

SOLUTION PAGE 249

## Sudoku Puzzle 48

| | | 2 | | 7 | | | | |
|---|---|---|---|---|---|---|---|---|
| 5 | 1 | | | 2 | | | 7 | |
| 7 | | | 4 | | | 2 | | |
| 3 | | | 6 | | | 4 | | 2 |
| | | | 9 | 5 | 7 | | | |
| 6 | | 1 | | | 3 | | | 8 |
| | | 7 | | | 4 | | | 9 |
| | 5 | | | 3 | | | 1 | 7 |
| | | | | 6 | | 5 | | |

SOLUTION PAGE 249

# Sudoku Puzzle 49

| | | | 7 | 2 | | 5 | 9 | |
|---|---|---|---|---|---|---|---|---|
| | 5 | | | | 1 | | 2 | 6 |
| 2 | | | | 5 | | 8 | | |
| | 7 | 5 | | | | | | 9 |
| 3 | | | | 9 | | | | 8 |
| 6 | | | | | | 1 | 5 | |
| | | 6 | | 7 | | | | 3 |
| 5 | 1 | | 8 | | | | 7 | |
| | 3 | 7 | | 1 | 6 | | | |

SOLUTION PAGE 250

# Sudoku Puzzle 50

| | | | 4 | | | | 6 | |
|---|---|---|---|---|---|---|---|---|
| 4 | | 1 | | 7 | 8 | | | |
| 8 | | | | | 2 | | 1 | 4 |
| 6 | | 9 | | | | | | 1 |
| 3 | | 8 | | 6 | | 7 | | 5 |
| 5 | | | | | | 4 | | 6 |
| 2 | 9 | | 5 | | | | | 8 |
| | | | 8 | 3 | | 1 | | 2 |
| | 8 | | | | 7 | | | |

SOLUTION PAGE 250

# Card Logic Puzzles

Card logic puzzles are designed to test your ability to decipher a pattern in a card arrangement. Here, figure out what card or cards are missing from the arrangement.

## Illustration

Two rows consisting of four cards each are laid out on a table. Each card in Row A corresponds to a card in Row B in some exact way. Knowing this, which card is missing from Row B?

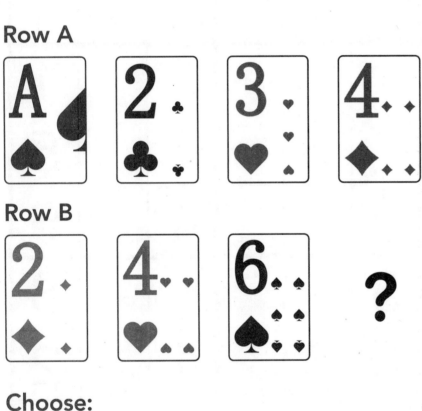

**Row A**

**Row B**

**Choose:**

A   B   C   D

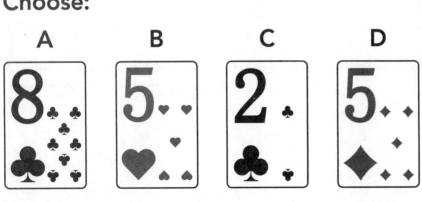

The answer is A. If you look carefully, you will see that the number value of each card in Row B is twice the one just above it in Row A. So below the four of diamonds in Row A, the missing card will have a number value of eight. Of the options given, only A works.

In the puzzles that follow, look out for these things: (a) the type of layout that is involved, (b) the location of the card in it, (c) the suit of the card, and (d) the number value of the card. Of course, not all of these are always involved in the solution.

# Card Logic Puzzle 1

Two rows of cards are laid out on a table. Which card is missing from the top row of the layout? **Hint:** Focus on the order of the cards in each row.

**Row A**

**Row B**

**Choose:**

| A | B | C | D |
|---|---|---|---|

# Card Logic Puzzle 2

Four hands have been dealt out to four different players from the standard fifty-two-card deck. The hands are shown in columns (from top to bottom). As it turns out, all four hands share an unexpected pattern. Which card is missing from the third hand? **Hint:** Each hand will have the same kinds of cards.

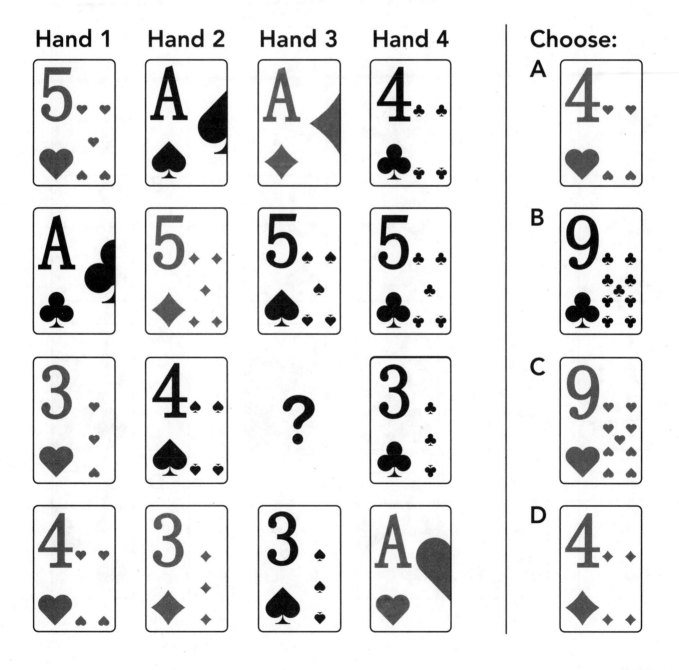

# Card Logic Puzzle 3

SOLUTION PAGE 251

The hands are shown in columns (from top to bottom). These four hands also share an unexpected pattern. Which card is missing from the fourth hand? **Hint:** Focus on the suits in each hand. Ignore the number values.

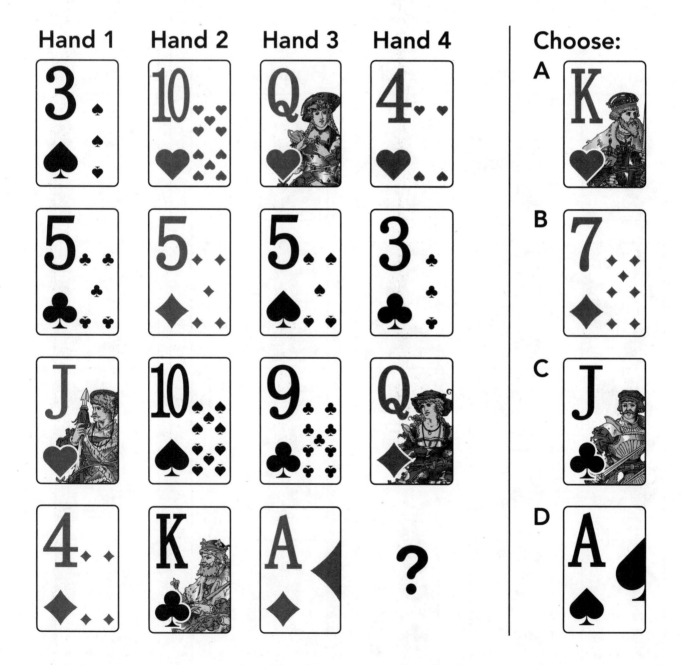

Hand 1  Hand 2  Hand 3  Hand 4  Choose:

The suit symbols are distributed in the following grid according to a system. Knowing this, which suit symbol is missing?

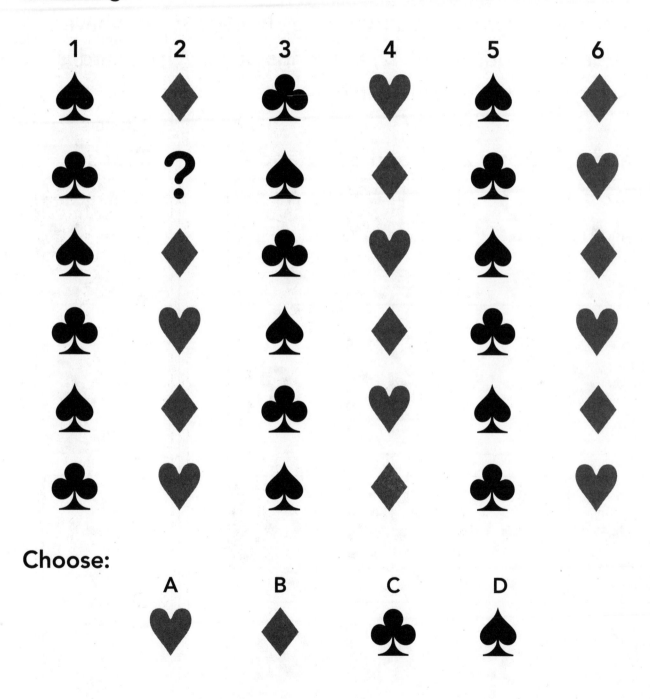

**Choose:**

A ♥  B ♦  C ♣  D ♠

Four hands are dealt from a standard fifty-two-card deck to four different players, and each hand is laid out in a separate column as shown. In each of the hands, there is the same pattern for you to unravel. Note that jacks have a value of 11, queens of 12, and kings of 13. Which card is missing from the fourth hand?

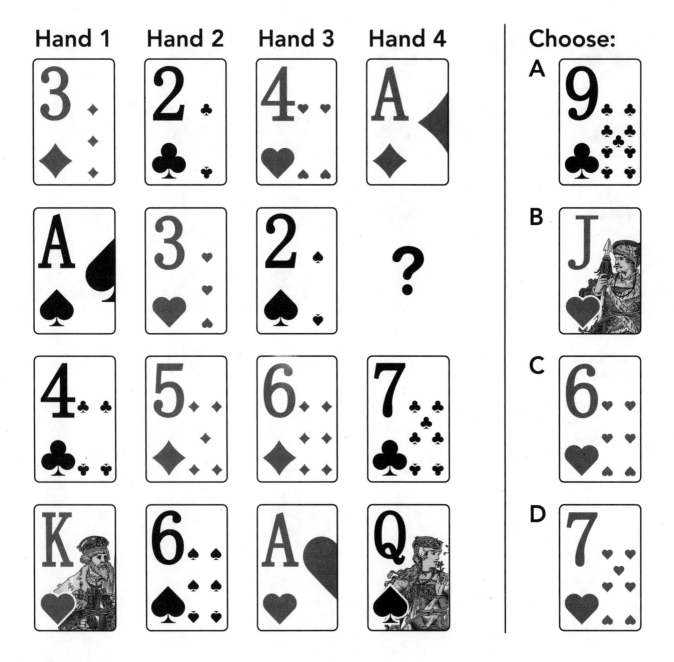

Hand 1   Hand 2   Hand 3   Hand 4     Choose:

A

B

C

D

# Card Logic Puzzle 6

SOLUTION PAGE 252

Four hands are dealt from a standard fifty-two-card deck to four different players. Each hand is laid out in a separate column. In each of the hands, there is an identical pattern for you to discover. Which card is missing from the first hand? Note that jacks have a value of 11, queens of 12, and kings of 13.

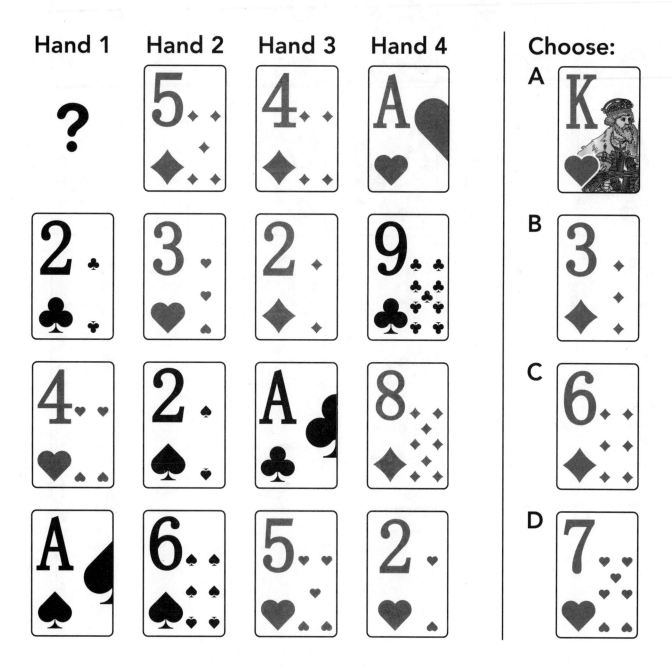

Hand 1  Hand 2  Hand 3  Hand 4  Choose:

A — K♥

B — 3♦

C — 6♦

D — 7♥

# Card Logic Puzzle 7

Sixteen cards have been inserted in the following grid in a systematic way. Can you figure out how they have been inserted?

| Set 1 | Set 2 | Set 3 | Set 4 |
|---|---|---|---|
| 2 ♠ | A ♥ | 2 ♣ | 5 ♦ |
| A ♠ | 4 ♥ | A ♣ | 6 ♦ |
| 3 ♠ | 2 ♥ | 4 ♣ | 9 ♦ |
| 4 ♠ | 3 ♥ | 3 ♣ | ? |

**Choose:**

A   10 ♦

B   9 ♣

C   6 ♠

D   8 ♦

**184**

# Domino Logic Puzzles

In these puzzles, the challenge is to identify a domino in a set or layout that does not belong there.

## Illustration

The dominoes in each column are placed there according to a rule. Which domino does not fit in?

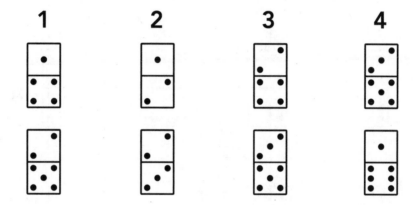

In each column a spot is added to the spots on the top and bottom parts of the first or top tile to produce the tile below it. So in the first column the top tile has one spot on its top part and four on its bottom part. The tile below it will have one more spot in each part—two spots on top and five on the bottom.

Look at the top tile in column 4. It has three spots on its top part and five spots on its bottom part. According to the rule, the bottom tile should have four spots on top and six on the bottom, but it has one on top and six on the bottom. So this is the odd domino out.

# Domino Logic Puzzle 1 SOLUTION PAGE 253

The following sequence of six dominoes constitutes a set—that is, each domino has a specific feature that allows it to belong in the set. But one does not. Can you detect it?
**Hint:** Look at the number of spots on the top and bottom parts of each tile—there is a constant relation between the two numbers in each tile, except one.

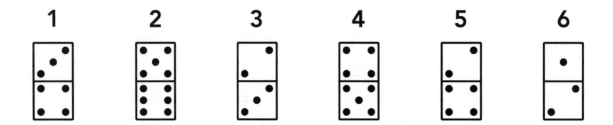

# Domino Logic Puzzle 2 SOLUTION PAGE 253

The following sequence has been constructed in a specific way, with each domino following the other according to a rule. But one does not. Which one is it? **Hint:** Look at how the number of spots on top and bottom progress one tile after the other.

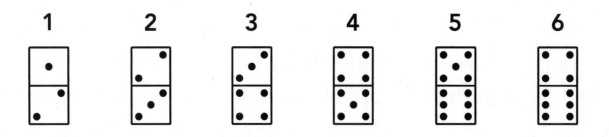

# Domino Logic Puzzle 3

SOLUTION PAGE 254

The dominoes in each column are placed there according to a rule. Which column does not fit in?

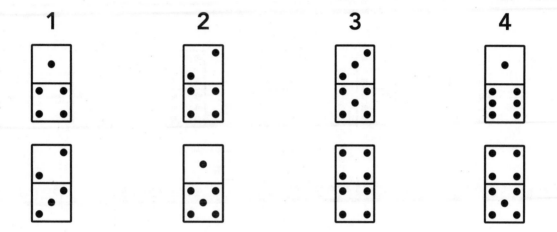

# Domino Logic Puzzle 4

SOLUTION PAGE 254

In the following set of dominoes, each tile except one displays a specific numerical pattern. Which one does not follow the pattern?

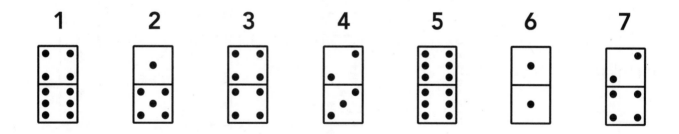

# Domino Logic Puzzle 5

SOLUTION PAGE 255

In this set of dominoes, each tile except one displays a specific numerical pattern. Which one does not follow the pattern?

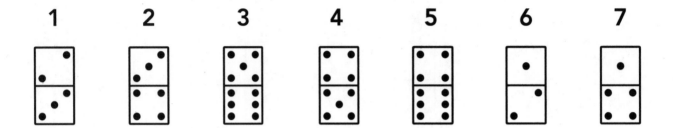

# Domino Logic Puzzle 6

SOLUTION PAGE 255

Four dominoes are placed in each of five columns. At the bottom of each column you will see a number. There is a pattern here. Which column is the odd one out?

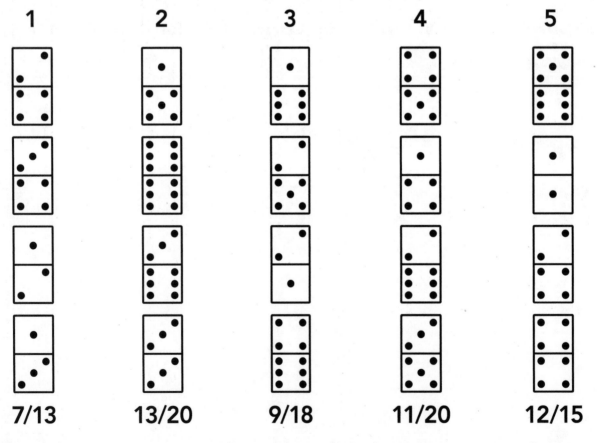

| 1 | 2 | 3 | 4 | 5 |
|---|---|---|---|---|
| 7/13 | 13/20 | 9/18 | 11/20 | 12/15 |

# Domino Logic Puzzle 7

Four dominoes are placed in each of five columns. At the bottom of each column you will see a number. There is a pattern here. Which column is the odd one out?

| 1 | 2 | 3 | 4 | 5 |
|---|---|---|---|---|

| 11 | 11 | 5 | 6 | 11 |
|---|---|---|---|---|

# Lie Detection Puzzles

Lie Detection Puzzles 1–10 involve five people who make statements to interrogators, some of which are true and others false. You are told exactly how many true and false statements there are in the set of five. Then, on the basis of these statements, you have to figure out—using logic—who the culprit is among the five.

## Illustration

Five gangsters were brought in for questioning. One was known to have murdered a gangster from another gang. Here's what each one said. As it turns out, three of the statements were true and two were false. Can you identify the killer on the basis of their statements?

| Dick: | I didn't do it. |
|---|---|
| Don: | Dick is innocent. |
| Dirk: | Dick didn't do it. |
| Dale: | Dick did it. |
| Devin: | I am innocent. |

Let's start with the first three statements. All three indicate the same thing, in different ways, of course— namely, that Dick is innocent. Dick declares his innocence outright, and the other two, Don and Dirk, agree. So these three statements are either all true or all false. We are told that there were three true statements and two false ones in the set. They cannot be all false because there were only two—not three—false ones. So we can safely deduce that they were all true.

This means that the remaining two statements, by Dale and Devin, were the false ones. Let's see what each one said. Dale said that Dick is the culprit. Well, this is false, as we just deduced. It changes nothing, so far. But look at Devin's statement. He says that he is innocent. This statement, as we now know, is one of the two false ones. Contrary to what he says, Devin is our killer.

# Lie Detection Puzzle 1

Five people were interrogated. One was known to have murdered an acquaintance. Here's what each one said. All the statements were true. Can you identify the killer?

| Andy: | I didn't do it. |
| Art: | I didn't do it either. |
| Alexa: | I didn't do it. |
| Ariana: | I am innocent. |
| Alina: | Alexa is innocent. |

# Lie Detection Puzzle 2

Five individuals were questioned. One was suspected of having robbed a bank. Here's what each one said. All the statements were false. Can you identify the robber?

| Bob: | Ben did it. |
| Brent: | No, Barb did it. |
| Bertha: | No, Bob did it. |
| Barb: | I don't know who did it. |
| Ben: | Bertha did it. |

# Lie Detection Puzzle 3

SOLUTION PAGE 257

Five workers from the same company were brought in for questioning. One was suspected of having embezzled company funds. Here's what each one said. Four statements were true and one was false. The false one was uttered by the embezzler. Can you identify the embezzler?

| Cam: | I didn't do it. |
|---|---|
| Charlotte: | Cam is innocent. |
| Carroll: | I didn't do it. |
| Claudia: | Carroll is innocent. |
| Chuck: | I didn't do it. |

# Lie Detection Puzzle 4

SOLUTION PAGE 258

Five gangsters were questioned by the police. One was suspected of having murdered a rival in another gang. Here's what each one said. Two statements were true and the other three were false. Strangely, the killer was one of the two who told the truth! Can you identify the killer?

| Evan: | Elvira did it. |
|---|---|
| Eric: | Evan lied. |
| Elana: | Elvira's the killer. |
| Emma: | Yeah, Elvira is the killer. |
| Elvira: | Evan lied. |

# Lie Detection Puzzle 5

SOLUTION PAGE 258

Five people were interrogated. One was suspected of having stolen money from a bank machine. Here's what each one said. Three statements were true and the other two were false. Can you identify the thief?

| Frank: | Felicia is the robber. |
|---|---|
| Fanny: | Faustus is the robber. |
| Filomena: | Frank is the robber. |
| Faustus: | I am innocent. |
| Felicia: | I am innocent. |

# Lie Detection Puzzle 6

SOLUTION PAGE 259

Five friends were interrogated. One was suspected of having murdered a paramour. Here's what each one said. Two statements were true and the other three were false. Can you identify the killer?

| Grant: | I didn't do it. |
|---|---|
| Glenda: | I didn't do it. |
| Gabby: | I didn't do it. |
| Gaston: | Glenda did it. |
| Gail: | Grant did it. |

# Lie Detection Puzzle 7

SOLUTION PAGE 259

Five colleagues were brought in for questioning. One was suspected of having murdered a coworker out of jealousy. Here's what each one said. Two statements were true and the other three were false. Can you identify the killer?

| Hank: | I didn't do it. |
|---|---|
| Helen: | Hank is innocent. |
| Harry: | I didn't do it. |
| Hanna: | I didn't do it. |
| Hubert: | Hank is innocent. |

# Lie Detection Puzzle 8

SOLUTION PAGE 260

Five coworkers were interrogated. One was suspected of having stolen company funds. Here's what each one said. Two statements were true and three were false. Can you identify the thief?

| Inez: | I didn't do it. |
|---|---|
| Irene: | Inez didn't do it. |
| Ida: | Ivan didn't do it. |
| Iris: | Inez did it. |
| Ivan: | Inez did it. |

# Lie Detection Puzzle 9

SOLUTION PAGE 260

Five renowned hackers were questioned. One was suspected of having hacked a top-secret government site. Here's what each one said. Three statements were true and two were false. The guilty hacker was actually one of the truth tellers. Can you identify the guilty hacker?

| Jack: | Jane is innocent. |
| Jane: | I am innocent. |
| Jim: | Jane did it. |
| Jenna: | Jack is innocent. |
| Jill: | Jane is innocent. |

# Lie Detection Puzzle 10

SOLUTION PAGE 261

Five people were interrogated. One was suspected of having murdered a romantic rival. Here's what each one said. Two statements were true and the other three were false. Can you identify the killer?

| Kyle: | I'm innocent. |
| Karen: | I'm innocent. |
| Ken: | Karen is the killer. |
| Kristina: | Kayla is innocent. |
| Kayla: | Kyle is the killer. |

In Puzzles 11 and 12, each person makes two statements, and you are told again how many statements are true or false. This variant adds more complexity to the kind of logic that is required.

## Illustration

Five people who all knew each other were interrogated. One was suspected of having murdered a secret romantic rival. Each one made two statements. Here are all the statements. There were eight true statements in total and two false ones. Can you identify the killer?

| Sam: | (1) Simon is innocent. |
|---|---|
| | (2) Shirley didn't do it. |
| Sarah: | (3) Shirley is innocent. |
| | (4) Simon is innocent. |
| Simon: | (5) I am innocent. |
| | (6) Sarah told the truth. |
| Shirley: | (7) Simon did it. |
| | (8) Sam didn't do it. |
| Sally: | (9) Shirley didn't do it. |
| | (10) Simon is innocent. |

Statements (2), (3), and (9) indicate the same thing—namely, that Shirley is innocent. These statements are thus all true or all false. They cannot be false because there were only two, not three, false statements in the set. Similar reasoning can be applied to statements (1), (5), and (10), which indicate the same thing—namely, that Simon is innocent. The three statements cannot be all false, since as we know there were only two false statements in the set. So they are true. And this means that Shirley and Simon are indeed innocent.

This makes six true statements so far. There were eight in total, so there were two other true statements in the set. Look at Sarah's statement (4). She says that Simon is innocent. As we just deduced, this is true. Next, look at Simon's statement (6). He says that Sarah told the truth, and she did by saying that both Shirley and Simon were innocent (as we deduced). We now have identified all eight true statements. This means that statements (7) and (8), both uttered by Shirley, are the two false ones. Her statement (7), "Simon did it," is clearly false. We know he is innocent. But her second statement (8), "Sam didn't do it," is also false. So, contrary to what she says, Sam is our culprit.

# Lie Detection Puzzle 11

SOLUTION PAGE 261

Five gangsters were interrogated. One was suspected of having murdered a rival gangster. Each one made two statements. Here are the statements, which were all true by the way. Can you identify the killer?

| Laura: | (1) I'm innocent. |
|--------|-------------------|
|        | (2) Lisa is innocent. |
| Lenny: | (3) I'm innocent. |
|        | (4) Linda is innocent. |
| Louise: | (5) Laura told the truth. |
|        | (6) So did Linda. |
| Linda: | (7) I'm innocent. |
|        | (8) Lenny is innocent. |
| Lisa: | (9) I'm innocent. |
|        | (10) Laura is innocent. |

# Lie Detection Puzzle 12

SOLUTION PAGE 262

Five individuals were interrogated. One was suspected of having robbed a local bank. Each one made two statements. Here are their statements. There were five true statements and five false ones. Interestingly, each individual made exactly one true and one false statement. Can you identify the robber?

| Shane: | (1) I didn't do it. |
| --- | --- |
| | (2) Steve did it. |
| Sheila: | (3) I didn't do it. |
| | (4) Samuel did it. |
| Samuel: | (5) There were five true statements. |
| | (6) Shane did it. |
| Steve: | (7) There were five false statements. |
| | (8) Sheila did it. |
| Sandra: | (9) Sheila is innocent. |
| | (10) I didn't do it. |

# Geometric Figure Puzzles

Geometric arithmetic puzzles are really arithmetic problems with geometric figures. You are given a number of equations from which a figure is missing in the last equation. You have to select the missing one using logic.

## Illustration

Here are four equations with geometric figures. Each figure stands for a specific number—that is, it has a specific numerical value. Find the missing figure.

$$\square \ + \ \triangle \ + \ \bigcirc \ = \ 8$$

$$\square \ - \ \bigcirc \ = \ 3$$

$$\triangle \ + \ \bigcirc \ = \ 4$$

$$\square \ - \ \bigcirc \ + \ ? \ = \ 6$$

What's the missing figure?

| A | B | C |
|---|---|---|
| $\square$ | $\triangle$ | $\bigcirc$ |

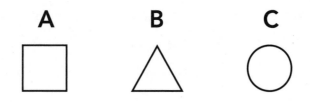

The answer is B. If you look carefully and compare the figures in the equations, you will see that the square stands for the number 4, the triangle for 3, and the circle for 1. Here are the numerical versions of the equations:

4 + 3 + 1 = 8
4 − 1 = 3
3 + 1 = 4
4 − 1 + 3 (missing) = 6

So the missing figure is the triangle, which stands for 3.

# Geometric Figure Puzzle 1 SOLUTION PAGE 262

Here are four equations with geometric figures. Each figure stands for a specific number—that is, it has a specific numerical value. Find the missing figure.

$$\square + \pentagon + \triangle = 9$$

$$\square + \square + \square + \square = 4$$

$$\pentagon - \triangle = 2$$

$$\pentagon + \mathbf{?} - \triangle = 7$$

What's the missing figure?

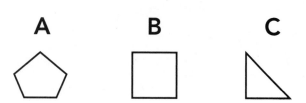

A     B     C

# Geometric Figure Puzzle 2 SOLUTION PAGE 263

Here are four equations with geometric figures. Each figure stands for a specific number. Find the missing figure.

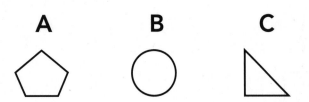

$$\text{⬠} \times \text{◺} - \text{◯} = 17$$
$$\text{◯} \times \text{◯} = 9$$
$$\text{⬠} \times \text{⬠} = 16$$
$$\text{⬠} + \text{◯} + \; ? \; = 10$$

What's the missing figure?

| A | B | C |
|---|---|---|
| ⬠ | ◯ | ◺ |

# Geometric Figure Puzzle 3 SOLUTION PAGE 263

Here are four equations with geometric figures. Each figure stands for a specific number. Find the missing figure.

$$\square + \square + \bigcirc + \bigcirc = 16$$

$$\square + \square + \bigcirc = 15$$

$$\triangle + \bigcirc + \bigcirc + \bigcirc = 6$$

$$\square + \bigcirc + \triangle + \;? = 18$$

What's the missing figure?

|     A     |     B     |     C     |
|:---------:|:---------:|:---------:|
| $\bigcirc$ | $\triangle$ | $\square$ |

# Geometric Figure Puzzle 4 SOLUTION PAGE 263

Here are four equations with geometric figures. Each figure stands for a specific number. Find the missing figure.

$$\bigcirc + \triangle + \square + \hexagon = 11$$

$$\square \times \hexagon \times \square = 5$$

$$\triangle + \triangle + \triangle = 9$$

$$\bigcirc + \square + \square + \,? \,= 9$$

What's the missing figure?

A $\bigcirc$    B $\square$    C $\triangle$    D $\hexagon$

# Geometric Figure Puzzle 5 SOLUTION PAGE 263

Here are five equations with geometric figures. Each figure stands for a specific number. For this puzzle you will have to provide the missing number (after the equation sign) rather than a missing figure. Find the missing number.

$$\text{box} \times \text{cylinder} = 6$$

$$\text{parallelogram} + \text{cylinder} = 3$$

$$\text{parallelogram} \times \text{cylinder} = 2$$

$$\text{box} \times \text{diamond} = 15$$

$$\text{box} + \text{cylinder} + \text{diamond} = \,?$$

What's the missing number?

| A | B | C | D |
|---|---|---|---|
| 4 | 8 | 12 | 10 |

Here are five equations with geometric figures. Each figure stands for a specific number. You will have to provide the missing number (after the equation sign) rather than a missing figure. Find the missing number.

Pentagon × Square = 8

Box × Circle = 3

Pentagon × Box = 12

Square × Circle = 2

Pentagon + Square + Box + Circle = **?**

What's the missing number?

| A | B | C | D |
|---|---|---|---|
| 10 | 12 | 6 | 9 |

# Geometric Figure Puzzle 7  SOLUTION PAGE 264

Here are five equations with geometric figures. Each figure stands for a specific number. You will have to provide the missing number (after the equation sign) rather than a missing figure. Find the missing number.

$$\text{(box)} \times \text{(square)} = 15$$

$$\text{(square)} + \text{(circle)} = 5$$

$$\text{(circle)} \times \text{(box)} = 10$$

$$\text{(square)} - \text{(pentagon)} = 2$$

$$\text{(box)} + \text{(square)} + \text{(pentagon)} + \text{(circle)} = \,?$$

What's the missing number?

| A | B | C | D |
|---|---|---|---|
| 9 | 10 | 11 | 12 |

# What's in the Boxes?

The classic type of box puzzle presents three boxes with wrong labels on them. You have to relabel them on the basis of logic alone, given certain information. Let's do one for the sake of illustration.

## Illustration

Three boxes, A, B, and C, contain fourteen billiard balls in total, colored blue or red. The boxes are labeled as shown, but the labels are wrong because someone had switched the labels on all three boxes. Can you figure out the correct labels if someone draws out a blue ball from Box B?

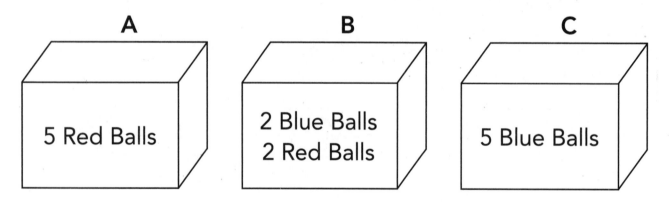

A
5 Red Balls

B
2 Blue Balls
2 Red Balls

C
5 Blue Balls

We know that Box B does not contain the two blue and two red balls, since it is mislabeled. So it has either the five red balls or the five blue balls. Because someone drew out a blue ball, we can now be sure that it contains the five blue balls. Let's show this as follows.

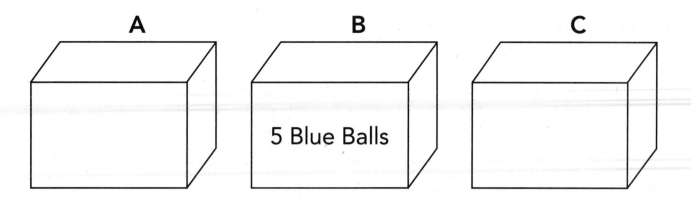

We know that A does not contain the five red balls because of the wrong label, nor does it contain the five blue balls (since we just deduced that B does); so it contains the two blue and two red balls (by process of elimination).

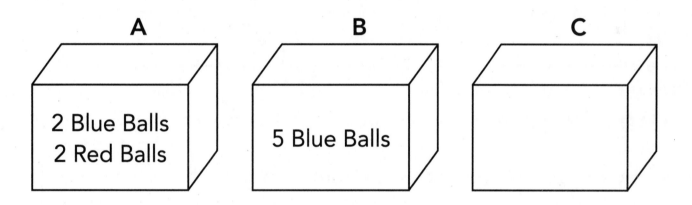

This means that the remaining five red balls are in Box C.

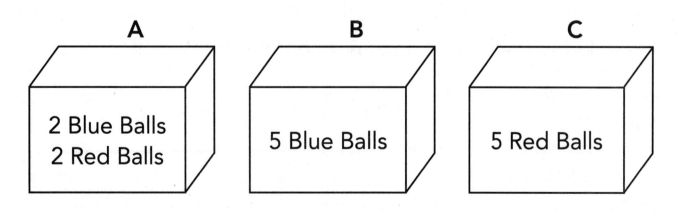

# Box Puzzle 1

SOLUTION PAGE 264

Three boxes, A, B, and C, contain five billiard balls in total, colored blue or red. The boxes are labeled as shown, but the labels are wrong because someone had switched the labels on all three boxes. Can you figure out the correct labels if someone draws out a blue ball from Box A?

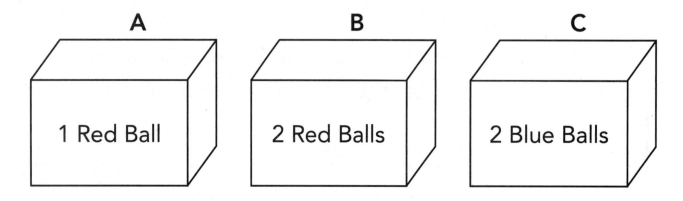

A

1 Red Ball

B

2 Red Balls

C

2 Blue Balls

# Box Puzzle 2

SOLUTION PAGE 264

Three boxes, A, B, and C, contain nine billiard balls in total, colored blue, red, or green. The boxes are labeled as shown, but the labels are wrong because someone had switched the labels on all three boxes. Can you figure out the correct labels if someone draws out a blue ball from Box A?

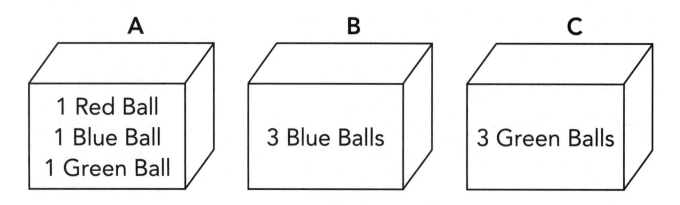

A

1 Red Ball
1 Blue Ball
1 Green Ball

B

3 Blue Balls

C

3 Green Balls

# Box Puzzle 3

SOLUTION PAGE 265

Three boxes, A, B, and C, contain sixteen billiard balls in total, colored blue, red, and green. The boxes are labeled as shown, but the labels are wrong because someone had switched the labels on all three boxes. Can you figure out the correct labels if someone draws out a green ball from Box B?

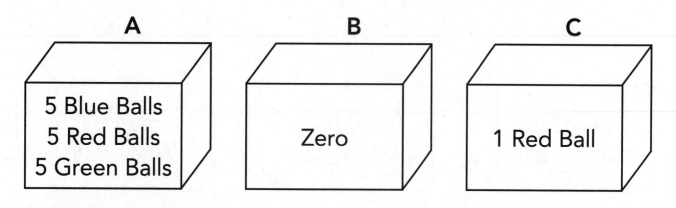

**A**

5 Blue Balls
5 Red Balls
5 Green Balls

**B**

Zero

**C**

1 Red Ball

# Box Puzzle 4

SOLUTION PAGE 265

Three boxes, A, B, and C, contain nine billiard balls in total, colored blue, red, and green. The boxes are labeled as shown, but the labels are wrong because someone had switched the labels on all three boxes. Can you figure out the correct labels if someone draws out three red balls from Box B?

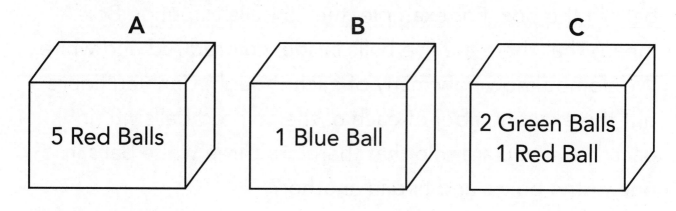

**A**

5 Red Balls

**B**

1 Blue Ball

**C**

2 Green Balls
1 Red Ball

# Box Puzzle 5

SOLUTION PAGE 266

Three boxes, A, B, and C, contain fourteen billiard balls in total, colored red, green, and white. The boxes are labeled as shown, but the labels are wrong because someone had switched the labels on all three boxes. Can you figure out the correct labels if someone draws out two red balls from Box C?

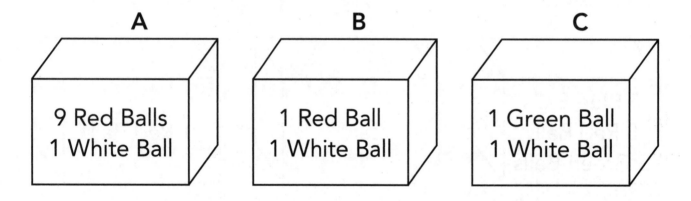

# Box Puzzle 6

SOLUTION PAGE 266

Three boxes, A, B, and C, contain ten billiard balls in total, colored red, green, and white. The boxes are labeled correctly this time but only indicate the colors of the balls within them, not the quantity of each colored ball. At the top of each box is a label indicating the total quantity of the balls in the box. For example, the "5 balls" label on Box A means that there are five balls inside, colored red and white. We do not know how many of each though. Can you figure out the exact number of each of the colored balls within each box if you are told that there are three white balls in one of the boxes and two in another?

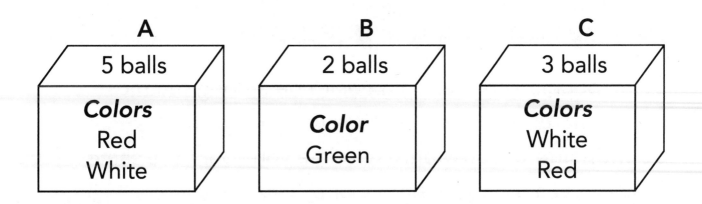

| A | B | C |
|---|---|---|
| 5 balls | 2 balls | 3 balls |
| **Colors**<br>Red<br>White | **Color**<br>Green | **Colors**<br>White<br>Red |

# Box Puzzle 7

SOLUTION PAGE 267

Three boxes, A, B, and C, contain eleven billiard balls in total, colored blue, red, green, and white. The boxes are labeled correctly but only indicate the colors of the balls within them, not the quantity of each colored ball. At the top of the box is a label indicating the total quantity of the balls in the box. Can you figure out the exact number of each colored ball within each box if you are told that there are three blue, three red, and three white balls in total?

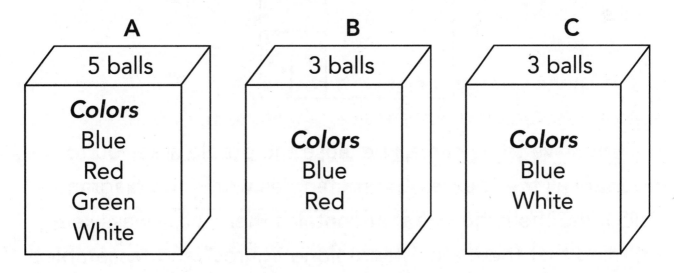

| A | B | C |
|---|---|---|
| 5 balls | 3 balls | 3 balls |
| **Colors**<br>Blue<br>Red<br>Green<br>White | **Colors**<br>Blue<br>Red | **Colors**<br>Blue<br>White |

# Figure-Counting Puzzles

Some people find these puzzles to be among the most frustrating of all types, since it is not unusual to come up with different answers each time you count the same figures. Let's try a very simple one.

## Illustration

This puzzle asks you to count how many complete four-sided figures (squares and rectangles) there are in the diagram altogether. A four-sided figure can be composed of smaller constituent figures, like pieces in a LEGO® set or a jigsaw puzzle.

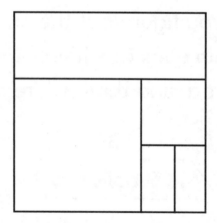

You have to be careful because the puzzle asks you to identify all the squares and rectangles within the diagram—including the large one that contains them all! Always keep in mind that there are "stand-alone figures" and "assembled figures." The best approach to these puzzles is to number all the segments you see. Let's start with the stand-alone figures.

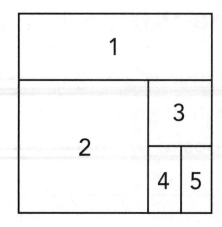

As you can see, figures 1, 2, 3, 4, and 5 are squares or rectangles that stand alone. Let's mark these down as follows.

### Stand-Alone Figures

1. 1
2. 2
3. 3
4. 4
5. 5

Let's now count the squares and rectangles that are assembled.

### Assembled Figures

6. 1 + 2 + 3 + 4 + 5 (These pieces make up the large square with all the internal figures. It is the easiest one to miss!)
7. 2 + 3 + 4 + 5
8. 3 + 4 + 5
9. 4 + 5

As you can see, there are nine four-sided figures in total—five stand-alones and four assembled figures.

# Figure-Counting Puzzle 1 SOLUTION PAGE 268

How many complete four-sided figures (squares and rectangles) are there in the following diagram altogether? A figure can be composed of smaller constituent figures.

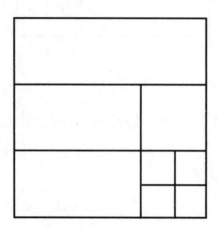

# Figure-Counting Puzzle 2 SOLUTION PAGE 269

How many complete triangles are there in the following diagram altogether? Note that a figure can be composed of smaller constituent figures.

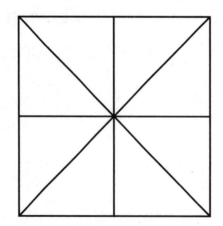

The last two puzzles involve figure counting but in a slightly different way. You will be asked to count how many triangles contain at least one circle. That's all there is to it. Let's do a very simple one for the sake of illustration.

## Illustration

In the following diagram, how many triangles, stand-alone and assembled, contain at least one circle? Note that a triangle can contain more than one circle in it.

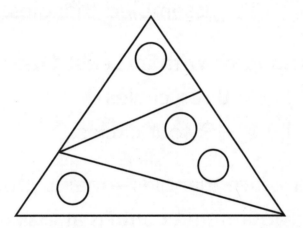

Let's number the diagram as in the previous puzzles for the sake of convenience. You must always keep in mind that there are stand-alone and assembled triangles in a diagram.

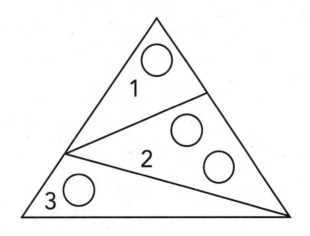

The stand-alones are 1, 2, and 3, and as you can see, each one has at least one circle in it—Triangle 2 has actually two of them. So far, therefore, three triangles contain at least one circle in them.

### Stand-Alones with at Least One Circle
1. Triangle 1: one circle
2. Triangle 2: two circles
3. Triangle 3: one circle

Now let's look at the assembled triangles.

### Assembled Triangles with at Least One Circle
4. Triangle 1 + 2: three circles
5. Triangle 1 + 2 + 3: four circles

So the answer is five triangles—that is, there are five triangles in the diagram that contain at least one circle in them.

# Figure-Counting Puzzle 3 SOLUTION PAGE 270

In the following diagram, how many triangles, stand-alone and assembled, contain at least one circle in them? Note that a triangle can contain more than one circle.

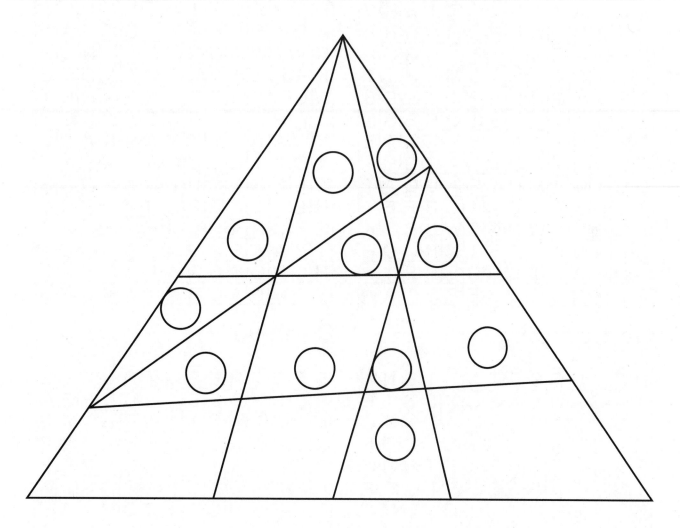

# Word Search Puzzle Answers

## Pet Friends

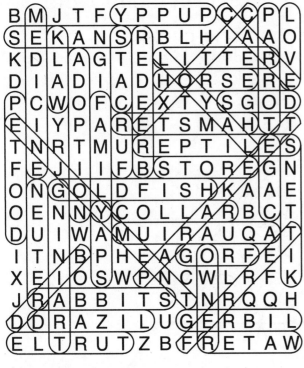

## Street Smart

## Go Camping

## Beehive

## Games

```
U A C B T X B R U L E S D P
N I W H L I S S E V O M L L
N V Y P E N M A F U N R U T
P I E C E S R E T N U O C G
O R P K I N S Y R D P H K Y
I T O S S C E N A R I O F B
N T G X H F T A B L E S R Y
T S P A C E S O D D P E I R
S O N M M S C R A B B L E R
R C V R O E E A I S E B N O
E F I L K N N L Q C A R D S
K U R D K Q O U E I X A S U
R E L I G O A P S I O M G O
A O D C S R Q O O O B B A V
M S L E E K T P L L Q Q U L
K S M L L F A M I L Y S F T
```

## School Time

```
T Y E X A M R M L I C N E P
E K F W I R E Y D U T S H R
A R X R M P A G S X R S V S
C O U I E A D L E U I G S U
H W M T D P I T O L P A B B
E E U I A E N C G H L M L J
R M L N C R G N A C C O A E
G O U G A L E S S O N S C C
P H C Q U I Z T S O D P K T
A C I T E M H T I R A M B E
V A R S I T Y T G L T A O G
P P R E C N A D N E T T A N
U P U T I C E G M C J H R U
P L C U U S S E C E R D O
I E T D K P R I N C I P A L
L R E D P E N U T K O O B R
```

## A Day at the Park

```
H C N E B L A N K E T I K J
M X B D P R E T L E H S Y M
Q O I G N I M M I W S E W Q
I B K E Q O G J O G G E R S
T D E O G H P E J N P Q H P
A N R N P M O U O L A A M L
B A S A O J G P A N D D A N
L S E C O G I Y S E S W E E
E S M U L B G S P C N V R R
S V R E C R E A T I O N C D
S G R E O E C T R N C T E L
A S N U W S B R A D A N C I
A R Q N I D O K R O K E L I H
G D S N W O L C A S S N P C
D G A M E S Z F O B E Z A G
L L I R G A P E D I L S C B
```

## Throw a Party

```
R A P P E T I Z E R S A P R
Y G R A D U A T I O N E E G
B I R T H D A Y V N O X N F
E T N E V E R H I P I I U T
S E N Y I C B V L M T D F E
I A O L T O E E G A A R C E
R P I I G R E C E P T I O N
P A T M S A A S K R I N C A
R R A A F T T P T J V K K G
U T R F O I R H K F N I T E
S Y B Y O O Y E E C I N A R
T S E L D N A C A R O G I S
S C L C I S U M S M I L L E
E U E H A L L O W E E N B M
U T C H R I S T M A S R G A
G R O U P B A L L O O N S G
```

## Powerful Words

```
B H H U S K Y S O U N D L L
E U U S E C U R E L B A T S
E N L N S E Y T N E T O P W
F K K K H E A L T H Y O V O
Y D I F Y K L B R A W N Y L
W U N O S N S E D E G G U R
W E R G R U N T I R I N G G O
N A N C O R O F D I L O S B
I B I E R A U H E F T Y A U
S L R F O L T R A W L A T S
T E U U G U Y D R U T S H T
E V D L I C F O R C I B L E
A I N A V S C A P A B L E G
D T E T G U I H C N U A T S
Y C F I R M I N Y T H G I M
N A B V E N E R G E T I C D
```

## Cute As a Button

## Little Gifts

## All Kinds of Toys

224

# Poker Games

```
B W Y K L B C D R O F X O M
Y I A W L D E D T H D I C Q
E N L W A U P D D L O H A A
T O P I C L A X U F A N C K
S R E E A A S Y J T A E C M
V D S P L B S T Z C S E D G
U G T A N F O I O G D U Q C
N E Y E S N F N N W N Q H J
D O M I X E D U G O S I U V
R R A Z Z A O M H L P E K Z
A H A N D C S M D S L G T X
C Y V W Y T Z O A B I D E H
V W N H U K U C A H T M B M
M I D G S B U T R I A P Q B
I A W F L U S H I G H G N V
O N W E V I F W V N W W W K
```

# Fun Fair

```
K S K E X H I B I T S Y B G
C O N C E S S I O N S G U A
O S S O T N I O C I S U M M
T S M S N O W C O N E S P E
S A A G R I C U L T U R E S
E P E N J T F U N H S Y R N
V E R I G I I O U A D T C O
I D C W B T V A C N O P A O
L I E S R E C N A D O I R L
I R C I L P V C R I G C S L
G W I T R M N D N C D T C A
H I I N O B B I R E U L B
T E Z G T C H E V A K R O D
S E J T P I Z Z A F A E W O
S C O N T E S T L T B S N O
G C S E C A R O U S E L S F
```

# Orbit

# Sing the Blues

## Play Tennis

```
S T E F A N E D B E R G A L
E H S A M S W L C U N R R C
R T B U A C E U S A T S J R
V J O L R T E O H H D I E O
E B R T T D P C U R M R S L
E O I F I E L R A M E N A A
O B S K N E A C Y D E N R N
R B B Z A S D C E T D D P D
N Y E H H L O F P R L R M G
E R C E I N R U E U O O A A
C I K W N E C A E O V P S R
M G E O G S G L M C E S E R
N G R O I A I M A T C H T O
H S R V S P I N G Y T O E S
O P A S S I N G S H O T P Z
J D I R A F A E L N A D A L
```

## At the Theater

```
U F U L I G H T S G S E T A
D N S M U S I C N E E G M D
T N H O G X E I Y A M A R D
I Y E E U N C A N A O T O J
C A R D E N I U O M V S F C
K L N R A A D D C E I N R S
E P Y D A R X I L N E E E N
T N I C D E K E A I W M P N
S R T T E N A N B C U T F G
T O R R N A S C E T E B A I
R C E E A E W E S S C S R N
A P C J D N V O A I S L E G
O O N R O T C E R I D L P M
T P O W O H S E X O B A O L
Q L C U R T A I N I U W B I
J S E H S G N I W C T J F F
```

## Christmas Display

```
S T T A W P O W E R E B I F
S W I T C H L L S Y N Y B R
A O S T J C R U T T E G A A
L A C P R E O E G H R B I T
G N C K M E F R B O G A O S
X I S I E A E B D L Y I N T
K M T L S T L G J I U H R D
S A E X U I N T W D W B S B
G T S P N I I E I A O A E I
C I M K R U S O M Y H T R L
Q O I T C U U P L A S T I C
C N S R O T H G I L N E W O
G N I H S A L F C P G R Z L
Y C L I U N R F U S E Y O O
L E D Y N R E K C I L F L R
H E G A T L O V U D C T R F
```

## Wedding Day

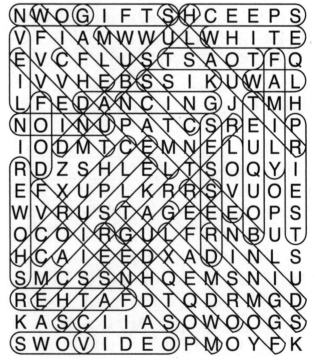

```
N W O G I F T S H C E E P S
V F I A M W W U L W H I T E
E V C F L U S T S A O T F Q
I V V H E B S S I K U W A L
L F E D A N C I N G J T M H
N O I N U P A T C S R E I P
I O D M T C E M N E L U L R
R D Z S H L E L T S O Q Y I
E F X U P L K R R S V U O E
W V R U S T A G E E E P S S
O C O I R G U L F R N B U T
H C A I E E D X A D I N L S
S M C S S N H Q E M S N I U
R E H T A F D T Q D R M G D
K A S C I I A S O W O O G S
S W O V I D E O P M O Y F K
```

## Start Your Engines

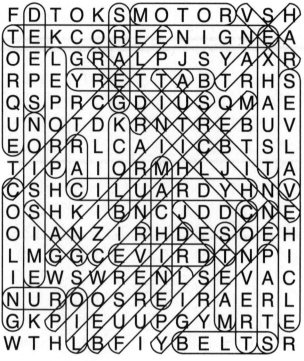

## On the Map

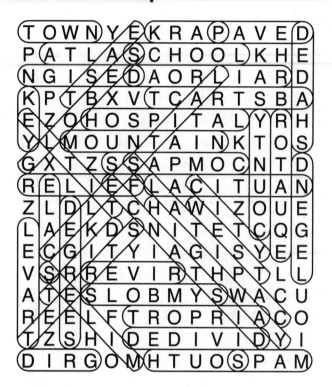

## Waterfall

## Carousel

## Silver Screen

```
L E U Q E S L G S B H J S S
E S H J D I P N T R C N R P
X I O R G O A I A O R J L R
T R A H P F U B R T I O C O
R W T C E O C B S I T Z R P
A S O O T R T U L D I M A S
S R G E G W U D N E C U C T
N N F N N A C T R E S S S U
T E K C I T F A A C T I O N
A F L O P T W F M E L C Y T
E M W N O H A N E E F A R S
M R A B O M B R P R R L E D
E O N R L F R A M E S A T A
H L R E D Y R T P I R C S E
T O V R G T N C O M E D Y L
R C X E Y R C P U E K A M Y
```

## Roots

```
G Q A W P A C Y D C R O P S
T M E U E N C R I A H N L D
V E N R H C D Q B R O M A N R
D B I K A H H S K R O Z N T
K A L D G O O E G O T Y N R
L C E U A R E A R T A N K E
E E I R B G N D E B T A X E
P C E H A E S A B I O T C L
L K A R T T P S U P P O R T
K I O F U A I H T B L B O F
H T O B R M X N T O W O T G
S N U S E U A G G O R O A M
D O N Z W E S Y R P O R D O
O I F O O D T G A H D T E A
P N J E L C I T S E R O F W
A O V R F D P I N R U T Q O
```

## Tasty

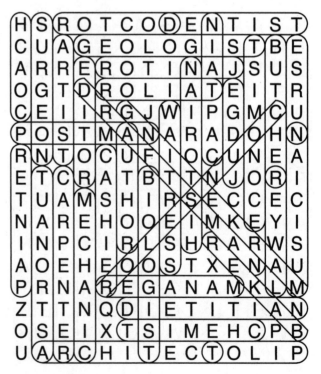

```
T R S H O R T B R E A D O S
N E I P Y R R E H C N U P C
I D F W O Y D N A C D R A H
M I X E D N U T S F U D G E
R C S B V E G G I E D I P E
E R T R A P P E T I Z E R S
P O U A P P L E C R I S P E
P C N N E B S I A A S M U C
E K T D C R N P N C K A M A
P C S Y A O O Y D A I E P K
I A E S N W O R Y R S R K E
C N H N P N R R C A S C I E
K D C A I I A E A M E E N F
L Y S P E E C B N E S C P F
E X V S T S A L E L B I O I
S W O L L A M H S R A M E T
```

## Get a Job

```
H S R O T C O D E N T I S T
C U A G E O L O G I S T B E
A R R E R O T I N A J S U S
O G T D R O L I A T E I T R
C E I I R G J W I P G M C U
P O S T M A N A R A D O H N
R N T O C U F I O C U N E A
E T C R A T B T T N J O R I
T U A M S H I R S E C C E C
N A R E H O O E I M K E Y I
I N P C I R L S H R A R W S
A O E H E O O S T X E N A U
P R N A R E G A N A M K L M
Z T T N Q D I E T I T I A N
O S E I X T S I M E H C P B
U A R C H I T E C T O L I P
```

228

## Have a Beer

## Fountain Pens

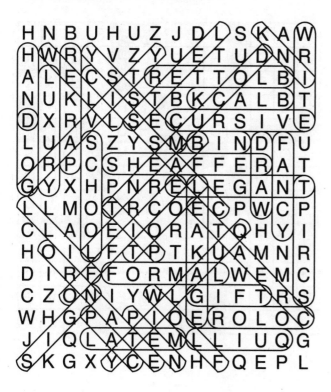

# Crossword Puzzle Answers

## Crossword Puzzle 1

```
A M O S   I D S   L O B E
S E A T   L E O   E V A N
A T T A   L A N   S A N G
N E S T L E   A I S L E
      E E G   R A E
W A G   N A T   M E S A S
E V A   L A S     A C T
E A S E D   N A M   T E N
      R E A   D O T
  S T A L L   N O O S E S
S H E S   A B E   A E R O
H O N E   R A S   S T A B
H O T S   M R S   T A S S
```

## Crossword Puzzle 3

```
H M O   E S C   M O U N T
B A N   S I P   A R T I E
O N E S T A R   R A I N S
      H E M     I N L E T
C A C H E     N O G
U S O   M E G A   E M M A
B A R   S A I N T   A I R
A P E D   C L U E   U R I
      H U H   R U L E D
H O G A N   P M S
E V E R T   O R I E N T S
F E R M I   N O T   A O K
T R I A L   O D E   G P A
```

## Crossword Puzzle 2

```
P O K E   S C O T   M I A
E K E S   T O D O   I T S
P I E S   R O S Y   S C H
  E L A T E S   A C H Y
    Y A P   R E X
C H A S M   G E N E T I C
B U S   A L O F T   I C U
S T A R L I T   R A C E D
    R E V   F A R
C A R S   C A P O T E
A P E   T O E S   M O N A
P A T   R U N T   A R C S
O L D   A R T S   S A L K
```

## Crossword Puzzle 4

```
C A N   A P P   S T E P
U S O   R A I L   T U B A
D I S   C I T E   A B B Y
  S E V E R   T R I E S
    I D S   H U N
R O A M   B A N   P J S
U A W   I D O L S   R E O
N F L   D E W   M E T S
    T O T   G S A
  P R O S E   A L I A S
M O A N   S O M E   S A M
R O V E   T I M E   I V E
I R I S   L A P   F E D
```

# Crossword Puzzle 5

```
A C C T   I S M     B L T
H O U R   I C Y   O A T H
M E T E   I O N   U N D O
E D E N     P A C T
    T R U E   E L B O W
T I C   O K S   L A R G E
A T H O M E   B E W A R E
C L A R A   F U R   N E D
O L D E N   E N Y A
    G O A D     C O M P
M I S O   M O B   I K E A
I T O N   F R Y   D I L L
C O W   M A E   S E T S
```

# Crossword Puzzle 7

```
M C S     A C T S   C C C
B L A B   I H O P   L O O
A O N E   R A T E   A D O
S T E E L   L O N   P E P
    N I K E   T N T
O L E   V A T S   P R A Y
R O L L E R   A F R A M E
B L E U   L A K E   P C T
    M G M   P E E P
A C E   I C E   S O R T S
V A N   T A M E   T O O L
O P T   T R A M   S I N O
N O S   S E N T   L E G
```

# Crossword Puzzle 6

```
T S P   C H A T     P I G
W O E   A B L Y   U R S A
O U R   R O S S   P O M P
  R U T H   O O H S
    W O K   N E E D Y
E S C A P E D   S T O O L
D U O   Y O U   T R I
U R B A N   A M A S S E D
  E B B E D   S T P
  H E E D   H Y M N
C O M O   C A F E   A I M
I N O R   O L I N   S C I
D A D   R Y E S   H E X
```

# Crossword Puzzle 8

```
G T O S   E Y E D   G P A
O H O H   D E C O   L A B
R A Z E   A T O Z   O R B
Y I E L D S   L E E W A Y
      O N L I N E
U P C   G E L   L A M B
M E O W   R A S   S U E T
P A P A   M A Y   G N U
    N E P A L I
B E A T L E   I N S E R T
T A B   L A C E   L U A U
U R L   I R O N   O R I G
S L Y   S L O T   G O D S
```

## Crossword Puzzle 9

```
P I G S . I W A S . M C S
A T I T . N O U N . A Y E
S O S A . T O G A . T S P
. . G R R . . R H E T T
S A L . N A U S E A . .
P S I . A N N E . S L O P
A W E S . S I N . P A P A
M E N U . I T S A . C A L
. . E S T E E M . K L M
T A S T E . . L Y E .
A L L . D I C E . B O S S
P E I . A I R S . B A K E
S G T . N I T S . S K I P
```

## Crossword Puzzle 11

```
D U D . O A R S . S U N
O H O H . F R E T . A P U
C O V E . T A D A . Y O N
S H E A R . B O G . O N S
. D I A L . S Y N .
C H I . F L E W . T A C T
O R N A T E . A N D R E A
P S A T . X E N A . A L T
. S A C . L E G S .
C H E . O W N . S T A S H
H A N . S A I D . A X E D
A N S . T I N A . B E R T
D D E . S L O B . L A V
```

## Crossword Puzzle 10

```
H E R E . S H A . S P I N
A D A M . M O S . C O C A
M U N I . A R K . O K A Y
. N H L . . L E N S
A P P E A L . M U D .
N A O M I . R I G . T A D
D I P . R H O D A . I C U
Y R S . D O W . N A K E D
. C O G . A D M I R E
C Z A R . M A O .
L A T E . C H E . E M M Y
O N I T . R U N . B R E D
P E P E . Y T D . A I D S
```

## Crossword Puzzle 12

```
B R A D . P A R . H M O S
R O L E . T I E . A U N T
A T T A . A M S . S L E D
S C A R F . S E N S E S .
. M A C . T E L .
A R R E A R S . D E N I M
H U T . O U R . O F A
A N E A R . P O L A R I S
. C A P . B O N .
N A C H O S . L I S P S
M O R E . S H A . M O A T
E A T S . T I M . A L L Y
W H Y S . S P A . L O S E
```

# Crossword Puzzle 13

| A | M | P | S | | | P | A | M | | | M | I | R |
|---|---|---|---|---|---|---|---|---|---|---|---|---|---|
| C | A | L | E | | | U | M | A | | | C | E | D | E |
| I | M | O | N | | | L | M | N | | | A | R | I | D |
| D | A | D | D | Y | L | O | N | G | L | E | G | S | |
| | | | S | A | T | | | A | T | L | | | |
| A | M | I | | | M | A | O | | | E | A | T | A | T |
| N | I | K | E | | | B | R | R | | | S | A | G | A |
| G | L | E | N | N | | | R | A | D | | | C | O | B |
| | | | C | O | D | | | M | S | G | | | |
| F | A | R | A | W | A | Y | P | L | A | C | E | S |
| R | I | B | S | | | R | E | A | | | P | U | L | P |
| E | R | I | E | | | T | A | G | | | E | R | M | A |
| D | E | S | | | S | H | E | | | S | L | O | T |

# Crossword Puzzle 15

| C | H | I | | | O | R | A | | | B | E | L | A |
|---|---|---|---|---|---|---|---|---|---|---|---|---|---|
| O | U | T | | | M | A | G | I | | | R | A | I | N |
| L | E | S | S | E | N | E | D | | | E | V | A | N |
| | | | I | N | K | | | C | I | N | E | M | A |
| S | T | I | R | S | | | L | A | D | D | | | |
| H | O | G | S | | | F | A | R | E | A | S | T |
| H | E | E | | | L | I | N | D | A | | | P | I | G |
| | | S | T | R | A | N | D | S | | | L | U | L | U |
| | | | A | L | A | S | | | S | I | R | E | N |
| R | A | G | T | A | G | | | M | A | O | | | |
| O | B | I | T | | | L | E | A | R | N | E | R | S |
| B | E | L | L | | | E | L | L | A | | | B | O | A |
| E | L | L | E | | | M | E | N | | | B | B | C |

# Crossword Puzzle 14

| D | E | C | O | | | S | L | I | T | | | L | B | S |
|---|---|---|---|---|---|---|---|---|---|---|---|---|---|---|
| O | A | H | U | | | T | I | N | A | | | I | O | U |
| I | S | I | T | | | A | L | E | C | | | V | A | N |
| T | E | A | S | E | R | | | R | I | S | E | R | S |
| | | | | G | R | O | T | T | O | | | |
| L | T | D | | | G | E | M | | | N | O | A | H |
| C | O | I | N | | | D | A | D | | | Y | O | Y | O |
| D | E | M | O | | | H | E | Y | | | H | E | W |
| | | | P | L | E | A | S | E | | | |
| A | P | P | E | A | R | | | I | N | T | A | C | T |
| J | A | R | | | L | I | A | R | | | E | Q | U | I |
| A | T | O | | | A | C | N | E | | | R | U | S | E |
| X | E | S | | | W | A | G | S | | | M | A | P | S |

# Crossword Puzzle 16

| F | B | I | | | A | L | T | A | | | A | M | B | I |
|---|---|---|---|---|---|---|---|---|---|---|---|---|---|---|
| C | A | N | | | G | A | R | B | | | L | O | A | N |
| C | R | T | | | I | N | O | R | | | L | O | R | D |
| | | N | E | I | L | D | I | A | M | O | N | D | |
| | | R | T | E | | | H | A | W | |
| A | S | E | C | | | D | A | S | | | S | C | I |
| M | U | S | H | R | O | O | M | C | L | O | U | D |
| P | E | T | | | A | R | T | | | Y | A | P | S |
| | | I | F | I | | | C | N | N | | |
| C | O | T | T | O | N | C | A | N | D | Y | |
| L | O | N | E | | | L | I | A | R | | | S | A | D |
| C | L | A | M | | | E | L | S | E | | | O | R | S |
| D | E | N | S | | | S | E | A | T | | | S | N | L |

# Crossword Puzzle 17

| L | I | M | O |   | U | P | C |   |   | F | E | B |
| I | M | A | C |   | S | I | D |   | A | L | V | A |
| M | U | T | T |   | H | E | R |   | C | U | E | S |
| A | S | H | O | R | E |   | O | T | H | E | R | S |
|   |   | P | A | R |   | M | O | O |   |   |   |   |
| M | A | R | I | N | E | R |   | M | O | R | A | L |
| E | S | P |   |   | D | R | S |   | A | P | O |   |
| L | I | M | I | T |   | S | C | E | N | E | R | Y |
|   |   | C | U | T |   | H | U | E |   |   |   |   |
| D | E | M | O | T | E |   | O | R | A | T | E | D |
| I | W | I | N |   | N | F | L |   | T | E | R | A |
| M | A | S | S |   | T | R | A |   | L | A | I | D |
| S | N | O |   |   | H | O | R |   | Y | M | C | A |

# Crossword Puzzle 19

| K | R | I | S |   | M | O | W |   | B | A | R | S |
| I | A | M | A |   | T | A | I |   | A | S | E | C |
| E | V | E | S |   | S | T | D |   | S | I | G | H |
| V | E | T | S |   |   | H | E | A | T |   |   |   |
|   |   |   | Y | A | P |   |   | S | E | A | L | S |
| L | M | N |   | L | E | A | D | S |   | G | O | O |
| E | E | E |   | T | E | P | E | E |   | U | A | W |
| F | R | I |   | A | L | T | E | R |   | E | D | S |
| T | E | N | O | R |   |   | P | T | S |   |   |   |
|   |   |   | U | S | S | R |   |   | P | F | F | T |
| B | I | T | S |   | P | O | W |   | A | L | I | E |
| C | O | A | T |   | E | A | R |   | S | E | R | A |
| D | U | D | S |   | D | R | Y |   | M | E | S | S |

# Crossword Puzzle 18

| M | A | T |   | O | F | F | S |   | S | T | E | P |
| R | Y | E |   | B | A | L | I |   | P | A | A | R |
| T | E | M | P | E | R | A | S |   | A | L | T | O |
|   |   |   | E | Y | E | S |   | P | R | E | S | S |
| M | A | S | T | S |   | H | A | R | E |   |   |   |
| I | A | T | E |   | S | I | N | E |   | N | R | A |
| S | H | O | R | T | A | N | D | S | W | E | E | T |
| S | S | W |   | O | C | T | A |   | A | M | F | M |
|   |   |   | R | U | S | H |   | C | L | O | S | E |
| L | A | S | E | R |   | E | G | A | D |   |   |   |
| A | N | N | S |   | E | P | I | S | O | D | E | S |
| S | K | I | T |   | P | A | S | T |   | R | E | P |
| S | A | P | S |   | A | N | T | E |   | S | K | Y |

# Crossword Puzzle 20

| L | O | T | T |   | A | S | I |   | B | I | D | S |
| E | U | R | O |   | T | K | O |   | U | T | A | H |
| I | S | O | N |   | L | A | T |   | T | O | N | Y |
| S | T | I | G | M | A |   | A | E | T | N | A |   |
|   |   |   | U | R | N |   | S | S | E |   |   |   |
| R | O | S | E | T | T | A |   | C | R | E | P | E |
| A | R | A | T |   | A | V | E |   | F | R | E | D |
| M | E | O | W | S |   | A | S | S | I | S | T | S |
|   |   |   | I | E | R |   | S | A | N |   |   |   |
|   | P | A | S | T | A |   | A | L | G | O | R | E |
| B | O | L | T |   | D | A | Y |   | E | B | A | Y |
| L | O | V | E |   | A | R | E |   | R | O | L | E |
| T | H | A | R |   | R | I | D |   | S | E | E | R |

# Crossword Puzzle 21

| C | R | O | P |   | L | O | L |   | C | E | L | L |
| H | O | H | O |   | I | F | I |   | R | I | C | O |
| A | L | M | S |   | B | A | T |   | A | N | D | Y |
| P | E | S | T | E | R |   | E | B | B |   |   |   |
|   |   |   | L | A | U | R | A |   | G | A | P |   |
| S | W | A | R | M |   | S | A | N | T | A | F | E |
| K | I | T | E |   | M | I | L |   | R | Y | A | N |
| I | R | O | N | M | A | N |   | T | I | E | R | S |
| P | E | P |   | A | R | G | U | E |   |   |   |   |
|   |   |   | P | C | T |   | N | E | S | T | E | D |
| S | I | Z | E |   | I | D | I |   | H | I | V | E |
| K | N | E | E |   | N | O | T |   | I | N | A | N |
| Y | A | N | K |   | I | C | Y |   | P | E | N | T |

# Crossword Puzzle 23

| A | G | O |   |   | I | C | U |   |   | S | S | E |
| N | A | R | C |   | R | A | S |   | S | E | A | L |
| A | L | S | O | R | A | N | S |   | T | A | L | K |
|   |   |   | U | R | S | A |   | D | O | M | E | S |
| E | P | I | C | S |   | D | I | N | O |   |   |   |
| T | E | S | H |   |   | I | T | A | L | I | A | N |
| T | E | M | P |   | H | A | S |   | P | A | G | E |
| A | L | S | O | R | A | N |   |   | I | M | E | T |
|   |   |   | T | O | M | B |   | E | G | A | D | S |
| S | P | R | A | Y |   | A | C | N | E |   |   |   |
| L | A | I | T |   | S | C | H | O | O | N | E | R |
| A | R | L | O |   | T | O | E |   | N | A | P | E |
| T | S | E |   |   | A | N | T |   |   | B | I | B |

# Crossword Puzzle 22

| P | T | A |   | S | O | F | A |   | A | C | D | C |
| Y | E | N |   | O | V | I | D |   | V | I | A | L |
| R | A | D |   | N | E | R | D |   | O | A | H | U |
| E | L | I | X | I | R |   | O | R | I | O | L | E |
|   |   | M | A | T |   | N | E | D |   |   |   |   |
| P | Y | L | E |   | M | T | V |   | D | D | S |   |
| J | O | A | N |   | L | E | O |   | L | O | O | P |
| S | U | P |   | F | E | W |   | O | H | M | Y |   |
|   |   | M | O | O |   | F | L | U |   |   |   |   |
| T | S | H | I | R | T |   | R | O | D | E | N | T |
| U | P | I | N |   | A | M | E | N |   | G | E | E |
| B | A | K | E |   | R | A | R | E |   | G | R | R |
| A | M | E | S |   | D | Y | E | R |   | Y | O | N |

# Crossword Puzzle 24

| C | R | A | M |   | P | U | B |   | A | L | U | M |
| S | I | R | E |   | E | S | E |   | R | A | Z | E |
| I | D | E | N | T | I | C | A | L | T | W | I | N |
|   | S | A | S | H |   |   | M | I | L |   |   |   |
|   |   | A | U | L | D |   | L | E | E | R | S |   |
| B | O | O |   | D | A | R | T |   | S | L | A | W |
| R | U | N | S |   | Y | E | S |   | S | E | G | A |
| A | C | C | T |   | S | A | A | B |   | V | E | T |
| S | H | E | A | F |   | M | R | E | D |   |   |   |
|   |   | T | O | M |   | T | O | U | T |   |   |   |
| E | P | L | U | R | I | B | U | S | U | N | U | M |
| L | E | A | R |   | N | A | M |   | S | I | N | O |
| F | A | M | E |   | E | S | S |   | E | X | A | M |

# Crossword Puzzle 25

```
T W I G . . U M S . A R C
A H E A D . P E R . N E A
T O R S O . P A S . K L M
. . . A C E D . . L A P .
M G M . . P R O . T E X .
A R A B I A . W H Y . . .
D E C A F . . E N R O N .
. . T S P . S M E A R S .
. N A H . A N I . F D A .
S O D . G I S T . . . . .
W O O . C O N . R O A R S
I S P . A D J . Y A H O O
G E T . B A A . R A M P .
```

# Crossword Puzzle 27

```
C C C . S T P . . S E N D
A P O . T I E S . O V I D
S A T . A C E T Y L E N E
A S T O N . N O V A . . .
. . O T C . . L E R N E R
A N N I E . W E S . E L O
F I G S . L E N . N A I L
A N I . M I T . O C T A L
R E N T A L . . R A F . .
. . . E R A S . T A R P S
I D O N T C A R E . E I N
S A W S . S L U G . A P U
P Y L E . . T E A . K E G
```

# Crossword Puzzle 26

```
U M P . . Z A P . . F D A
G O O F . U S A . S E A L
H E E L . L A M . P E R M
. . . E M U . M I L E S .
O W N E R . O T I C . . .
R O O T S . D O T E L L .
B E G . C O W . . Y A Y .
. S O O N E R . G E N R E
. . G A L S . O I N K S .
S H A R P . . G T E . . .
T U B E . C R O . I N F O
O R B S . H I D . O I L Y
P L Y . . A B S . . H A L
```

# Crossword Puzzle 28

```
S P F . I F S . D E V I L
L O A . N I H . O P I N E
U P I . D R Y . D I S C O
M E R C I . . . G L E A N
. . . B A S . C E O . . .
A Y E S . T H Y . G A L L
D E N . R E C . . P I T .
J A V A . A W L . S P U D
. N N W . E E K . . . . .
T O N T O . . . V I S T A
A T O L L . B Y E . T E L
B I N E T . B O N . A S P
S C O R E . C U T . G T O
```

# Crossword Puzzle 29

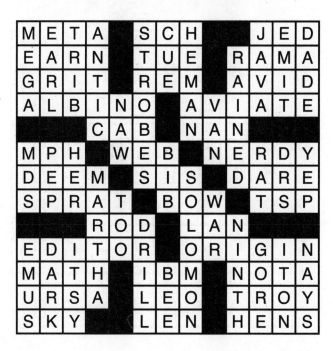

| | | | | | | | | | | | |
|---|---|---|---|---|---|---|---|---|---|---|---|
| H | U | G | S | ■ | U | F | O | S | ■ | L | I | P |
| I | N | A | N | ■ | T | R | A | P | ■ | E | V | A |
| S | O | L | I | T | A | I | R | E | ■ | M | A | T |
| ■ | ■ | D | U | H | ■ | ■ | C | L | O | N | E | |
| P | O | S | E | R | ■ | O | R | S | O | N | ■ | |
| A | R | M | ■ | F | I | N | E | ■ | A | L | F | A |
| I | C | E | D | ■ | Z | E | E | ■ | M | A | I | M |
| D | A | L | E | ■ | O | A | K | S | ■ | W | R | Y |
| ■ | ■ | L | E | N | D | L | ■ | N | O | S | E | S |
| A | T | A | R | I | ■ | ■ | P | A | R | ■ | ■ | |
| B | U | R | ■ | C | A | N | O | P | E | N | E | R |
| E | R | A | ■ | E | K | E | D | ■ | O | B | E | Y |
| T | N | T | ■ | R | A | T | S | ■ | S | A | K | E |

# Crossword Puzzle 30

| | | | | | | | | | | | |
|---|---|---|---|---|---|---|---|---|---|---|---|
| M | E | T | A | ■ | S | C | H | ■ | J | E | D | |
| E | A | R | N | ■ | T | U | E | ■ | R | A | M | A |
| G | R | I | T | ■ | R | E | M | ■ | A | V | I | D |
| A | L | B | I | N | O | ■ | A | V | I | A | T | E |
| ■ | ■ | C | A | B | ■ | N | A | N | ■ | ■ | ■ | |
| M | P | H | ■ | W | E | B | ■ | N | E | R | D | Y |
| D | E | E | M | ■ | S | I | S | ■ | D | A | R | E |
| S | P | R | A | T | ■ | B | O | W | ■ | T | S | P |
| ■ | ■ | R | O | D | ■ | L | A | N | ■ | ■ | ■ | |
| E | D | I | T | O | R | ■ | O | R | I | G | I | N |
| M | A | T | H | ■ | I | B | M | ■ | N | O | T | A |
| U | R | S | A | ■ | L | E | O | ■ | T | R | O | Y |
| S | K | Y | ■ | L | E | N | ■ | H | E | N | S | |

# Sudoku Puzzle Answers

## Sudoku Puzzle 1

| 5 | 2 | 4 | 9 | 6 | 7 | 8 | 3 | 1 |
|---|---|---|---|---|---|---|---|---|
| 3 | 7 | 8 | 2 | 5 | 1 | 4 | 6 | 9 |
| 1 | 6 | 9 | 4 | 8 | 3 | 2 | 5 | 7 |
| 6 | 8 | 2 | 7 | 9 | 5 | 3 | 1 | 4 |
| 9 | 4 | 3 | 1 | 2 | 8 | 6 | 7 | 5 |
| 7 | 1 | 5 | 6 | 3 | 4 | 9 | 8 | 2 |
| 4 | 5 | 6 | 3 | 7 | 9 | 1 | 2 | 8 |
| 8 | 3 | 1 | 5 | 4 | 2 | 7 | 9 | 6 |
| 2 | 9 | 7 | 8 | 1 | 6 | 5 | 4 | 3 |

## Sudoku Puzzle 3

| 4 | 9 | 5 | 3 | 1 | 6 | 7 | 2 | 8 |
|---|---|---|---|---|---|---|---|---|
| 3 | 7 | 1 | 4 | 8 | 2 | 6 | 5 | 9 |
| 2 | 6 | 8 | 7 | 9 | 5 | 1 | 4 | 3 |
| 6 | 4 | 2 | 9 | 3 | 1 | 8 | 7 | 5 |
| 7 | 1 | 3 | 5 | 2 | 8 | 4 | 9 | 6 |
| 5 | 8 | 9 | 6 | 7 | 4 | 2 | 3 | 1 |
| 8 | 5 | 4 | 2 | 6 | 9 | 3 | 1 | 7 |
| 9 | 3 | 6 | 1 | 4 | 7 | 5 | 8 | 2 |
| 1 | 2 | 7 | 8 | 5 | 3 | 9 | 6 | 4 |

## Sudoku Puzzle 2

| 9 | 1 | 3 | 4 | 8 | 6 | 5 | 2 | 7 |
|---|---|---|---|---|---|---|---|---|
| 2 | 4 | 8 | 3 | 5 | 7 | 1 | 6 | 9 |
| 5 | 6 | 7 | 9 | 1 | 2 | 4 | 3 | 8 |
| 1 | 8 | 5 | 6 | 4 | 3 | 7 | 9 | 2 |
| 4 | 9 | 6 | 2 | 7 | 8 | 3 | 5 | 1 |
| 7 | 3 | 2 | 1 | 9 | 5 | 6 | 8 | 4 |
| 6 | 7 | 9 | 5 | 2 | 1 | 8 | 4 | 3 |
| 3 | 2 | 1 | 8 | 6 | 4 | 9 | 7 | 5 |
| 8 | 5 | 4 | 7 | 3 | 9 | 2 | 1 | 6 |

## Sudoku Puzzle 4

| 2 | 9 | 8 | 1 | 7 | 5 | 6 | 3 | 4 |
|---|---|---|---|---|---|---|---|---|
| 6 | 5 | 4 | 3 | 9 | 2 | 7 | 8 | 1 |
| 3 | 1 | 7 | 4 | 6 | 8 | 5 | 9 | 2 |
| 9 | 3 | 2 | 5 | 1 | 7 | 8 | 4 | 6 |
| 4 | 6 | 1 | 8 | 2 | 3 | 9 | 7 | 5 |
| 7 | 8 | 5 | 6 | 4 | 9 | 2 | 1 | 3 |
| 8 | 4 | 6 | 7 | 5 | 1 | 3 | 2 | 9 |
| 1 | 2 | 3 | 9 | 8 | 6 | 4 | 5 | 7 |
| 5 | 7 | 9 | 2 | 3 | 4 | 1 | 6 | 8 |

## Sudoku Puzzle 5

| 9 | 6 | 7 | 2 | 3 | 8 | 4 | 5 | 1 |
|---|---|---|---|---|---|---|---|---|
| 2 | 1 | 8 | 6 | 4 | 5 | 9 | 7 | 3 |
| 3 | 4 | 5 | 7 | 9 | 1 | 6 | 2 | 8 |
| 6 | 3 | 1 | 9 | 8 | 2 | 5 | 4 | 7 |
| 8 | 5 | 9 | 1 | 7 | 4 | 3 | 6 | 2 |
| 4 | 7 | 2 | 5 | 6 | 3 | 1 | 8 | 9 |
| 1 | 8 | 3 | 4 | 5 | 7 | 2 | 9 | 6 |
| 5 | 2 | 6 | 8 | 1 | 9 | 7 | 3 | 4 |
| 7 | 9 | 4 | 3 | 2 | 6 | 8 | 1 | 5 |

## Sudoku Puzzle 7

| 8 | 9 | 7 | 5 | 3 | 6 | 4 | 1 | 2 |
|---|---|---|---|---|---|---|---|---|
| 6 | 3 | 2 | 1 | 4 | 8 | 5 | 7 | 9 |
| 4 | 1 | 5 | 2 | 7 | 9 | 8 | 3 | 6 |
| 5 | 6 | 4 | 7 | 2 | 3 | 9 | 8 | 1 |
| 3 | 2 | 1 | 9 | 8 | 4 | 7 | 6 | 5 |
| 9 | 7 | 8 | 6 | 1 | 5 | 3 | 2 | 4 |
| 2 | 5 | 6 | 8 | 9 | 7 | 1 | 4 | 3 |
| 1 | 8 | 3 | 4 | 5 | 2 | 6 | 9 | 7 |
| 7 | 4 | 9 | 3 | 6 | 1 | 2 | 5 | 8 |

## Sudoku Puzzle 6

| 4 | 5 | 7 | 1 | 9 | 6 | 8 | 3 | 2 |
|---|---|---|---|---|---|---|---|---|
| 1 | 8 | 2 | 7 | 3 | 5 | 9 | 6 | 4 |
| 9 | 6 | 3 | 8 | 4 | 2 | 1 | 7 | 5 |
| 5 | 7 | 1 | 4 | 8 | 9 | 3 | 2 | 6 |
| 3 | 2 | 8 | 6 | 1 | 7 | 5 | 4 | 9 |
| 6 | 9 | 4 | 2 | 5 | 3 | 7 | 8 | 1 |
| 2 | 1 | 9 | 3 | 6 | 8 | 4 | 5 | 7 |
| 7 | 3 | 5 | 9 | 2 | 4 | 6 | 1 | 8 |
| 8 | 4 | 6 | 5 | 7 | 1 | 2 | 9 | 3 |

## Sudoku Puzzle 8

| 8 | 9 | 7 | 1 | 3 | 4 | 6 | 2 | 5 |
|---|---|---|---|---|---|---|---|---|
| 5 | 4 | 6 | 7 | 2 | 8 | 1 | 9 | 3 |
| 3 | 1 | 2 | 9 | 5 | 6 | 8 | 4 | 7 |
| 6 | 7 | 3 | 4 | 1 | 2 | 5 | 8 | 9 |
| 9 | 5 | 4 | 3 | 8 | 7 | 2 | 1 | 6 |
| 1 | 2 | 8 | 5 | 6 | 9 | 3 | 7 | 4 |
| 7 | 6 | 1 | 8 | 9 | 3 | 4 | 5 | 2 |
| 2 | 8 | 9 | 6 | 4 | 5 | 7 | 3 | 1 |
| 4 | 3 | 5 | 2 | 7 | 1 | 9 | 6 | 8 |

## Sudoku Puzzle 9

| 8 | 9 | 7 | 6 | 5 | 2 | 4 | 1 | 3 |
|---|---|---|---|---|---|---|---|---|
| 3 | 6 | 2 | 1 | 4 | 8 | 9 | 7 | 5 |
| 4 | 5 | 1 | 7 | 3 | 9 | 2 | 6 | 8 |
| 6 | 3 | 4 | 9 | 8 | 5 | 7 | 2 | 1 |
| 7 | 1 | 9 | 2 | 6 | 3 | 8 | 5 | 4 |
| 2 | 8 | 5 | 4 | 1 | 7 | 6 | 3 | 9 |
| 5 | 7 | 6 | 8 | 9 | 1 | 3 | 4 | 2 |
| 9 | 4 | 3 | 5 | 2 | 6 | 1 | 8 | 7 |
| 1 | 2 | 8 | 3 | 7 | 4 | 5 | 9 | 6 |

## Sudoku Puzzle 11

| 9 | 6 | 2 | 4 | 8 | 3 | 1 | 7 | 5 |
|---|---|---|---|---|---|---|---|---|
| 8 | 7 | 5 | 2 | 1 | 6 | 4 | 9 | 3 |
| 3 | 1 | 4 | 7 | 5 | 9 | 8 | 6 | 2 |
| 1 | 8 | 7 | 9 | 4 | 5 | 3 | 2 | 6 |
| 6 | 5 | 3 | 8 | 2 | 7 | 9 | 4 | 1 |
| 4 | 2 | 9 | 3 | 6 | 1 | 7 | 5 | 8 |
| 5 | 3 | 6 | 1 | 9 | 4 | 2 | 8 | 7 |
| 7 | 4 | 8 | 5 | 3 | 2 | 6 | 1 | 9 |
| 2 | 9 | 1 | 6 | 7 | 8 | 5 | 3 | 4 |

## Sudoku Puzzle 10

| 6 | 2 | 8 | 7 | 9 | 1 | 3 | 5 | 4 |
|---|---|---|---|---|---|---|---|---|
| 1 | 3 | 4 | 8 | 6 | 5 | 7 | 2 | 9 |
| 7 | 9 | 5 | 4 | 3 | 2 | 8 | 6 | 1 |
| 5 | 1 | 7 | 9 | 4 | 8 | 6 | 3 | 2 |
| 9 | 4 | 3 | 5 | 2 | 6 | 1 | 8 | 7 |
| 2 | 8 | 6 | 3 | 1 | 7 | 9 | 4 | 5 |
| 8 | 7 | 1 | 2 | 5 | 3 | 4 | 9 | 6 |
| 3 | 5 | 9 | 6 | 7 | 4 | 2 | 1 | 8 |
| 4 | 6 | 2 | 1 | 8 | 9 | 5 | 7 | 3 |

## Sudoku Puzzle 12

| 4 | 5 | 9 | 3 | 2 | 8 | 7 | 1 | 6 |
|---|---|---|---|---|---|---|---|---|
| 6 | 1 | 7 | 5 | 9 | 4 | 3 | 8 | 2 |
| 2 | 3 | 8 | 7 | 1 | 6 | 4 | 5 | 9 |
| 9 | 6 | 3 | 8 | 5 | 1 | 2 | 7 | 4 |
| 1 | 7 | 2 | 6 | 4 | 9 | 8 | 3 | 5 |
| 8 | 4 | 5 | 2 | 3 | 7 | 6 | 9 | 1 |
| 3 | 9 | 1 | 4 | 7 | 2 | 5 | 6 | 8 |
| 5 | 2 | 6 | 1 | 8 | 3 | 9 | 4 | 7 |
| 7 | 8 | 4 | 9 | 6 | 5 | 1 | 2 | 3 |

## Sudoku Puzzle 13

| 6 | 7 | 8 | 4 | 9 | 2 | 3 | 5 | 1 |
| 4 | 3 | 5 | 7 | 8 | 1 | 9 | 6 | 2 |
| 1 | 2 | 9 | 5 | 6 | 3 | 7 | 4 | 8 |
| 2 | 8 | 7 | 9 | 1 | 4 | 5 | 3 | 6 |
| 3 | 5 | 4 | 6 | 2 | 8 | 1 | 7 | 9 |
| 9 | 6 | 1 | 3 | 7 | 5 | 8 | 2 | 4 |
| 8 | 1 | 6 | 2 | 3 | 7 | 4 | 9 | 5 |
| 7 | 4 | 2 | 8 | 5 | 9 | 6 | 1 | 3 |
| 5 | 9 | 3 | 1 | 4 | 6 | 2 | 8 | 7 |

## Sudoku Puzzle 15

| 3 | 8 | 7 | 5 | 6 | 9 | 4 | 1 | 2 |
| 5 | 2 | 1 | 3 | 8 | 4 | 7 | 6 | 9 |
| 4 | 6 | 9 | 7 | 2 | 1 | 5 | 3 | 8 |
| 9 | 1 | 6 | 4 | 7 | 8 | 3 | 2 | 5 |
| 2 | 3 | 8 | 1 | 9 | 5 | 6 | 4 | 7 |
| 7 | 5 | 4 | 6 | 3 | 2 | 9 | 8 | 1 |
| 6 | 4 | 5 | 2 | 1 | 7 | 8 | 9 | 3 |
| 1 | 9 | 3 | 8 | 5 | 6 | 2 | 7 | 4 |
| 8 | 7 | 2 | 9 | 4 | 3 | 1 | 5 | 6 |

## Sudoku Puzzle 14

| 4 | 9 | 1 | 7 | 8 | 5 | 6 | 2 | 3 |
| 5 | 3 | 6 | 9 | 2 | 1 | 4 | 7 | 8 |
| 7 | 8 | 2 | 6 | 3 | 4 | 1 | 9 | 5 |
| 3 | 6 | 8 | 1 | 4 | 9 | 7 | 5 | 2 |
| 2 | 1 | 7 | 8 | 5 | 6 | 9 | 3 | 4 |
| 9 | 4 | 5 | 2 | 7 | 3 | 8 | 1 | 6 |
| 1 | 2 | 9 | 5 | 6 | 8 | 3 | 4 | 7 |
| 8 | 5 | 4 | 3 | 1 | 7 | 2 | 6 | 9 |
| 6 | 7 | 3 | 4 | 9 | 2 | 5 | 8 | 1 |

## Sudoku Puzzle 16

| 1 | 5 | 2 | 9 | 4 | 7 | 3 | 6 | 8 |
| 3 | 4 | 6 | 2 | 8 | 1 | 9 | 7 | 5 |
| 8 | 9 | 7 | 5 | 3 | 6 | 2 | 1 | 4 |
| 4 | 2 | 8 | 1 | 7 | 5 | 6 | 9 | 3 |
| 9 | 3 | 1 | 4 | 6 | 8 | 5 | 2 | 7 |
| 6 | 7 | 5 | 3 | 9 | 2 | 4 | 8 | 1 |
| 5 | 1 | 4 | 7 | 2 | 9 | 8 | 3 | 6 |
| 7 | 6 | 9 | 8 | 5 | 3 | 1 | 4 | 2 |
| 2 | 8 | 3 | 6 | 1 | 4 | 7 | 5 | 9 |

## Sudoku Puzzle 17

| 9 | 6 | 3 | 7 | 8 | 5 | 4 | 2 | 1 |
|---|---|---|---|---|---|---|---|---|
| 1 | 5 | 7 | 2 | 6 | 4 | 3 | 9 | 8 |
| 8 | 2 | 4 | 3 | 9 | 1 | 7 | 6 | 5 |
| 5 | 4 | 8 | 6 | 2 | 3 | 1 | 7 | 9 |
| 7 | 1 | 9 | 5 | 4 | 8 | 2 | 3 | 6 |
| 2 | 3 | 6 | 9 | 1 | 7 | 5 | 8 | 4 |
| 4 | 7 | 2 | 8 | 5 | 9 | 6 | 1 | 3 |
| 6 | 9 | 1 | 4 | 3 | 2 | 8 | 5 | 7 |
| 3 | 8 | 5 | 1 | 7 | 6 | 9 | 4 | 2 |

## Sudoku Puzzle 19

| 1 | 5 | 3 | 8 | 4 | 6 | 2 | 9 | 7 |
|---|---|---|---|---|---|---|---|---|
| 6 | 7 | 2 | 1 | 3 | 9 | 4 | 8 | 5 |
| 9 | 4 | 8 | 5 | 2 | 7 | 6 | 3 | 1 |
| 8 | 6 | 4 | 9 | 1 | 5 | 7 | 2 | 3 |
| 3 | 1 | 9 | 7 | 8 | 2 | 5 | 6 | 4 |
| 5 | 2 | 7 | 4 | 6 | 3 | 8 | 1 | 9 |
| 2 | 9 | 6 | 3 | 7 | 4 | 1 | 5 | 8 |
| 7 | 3 | 1 | 2 | 5 | 8 | 9 | 4 | 6 |
| 4 | 8 | 5 | 6 | 9 | 1 | 3 | 7 | 2 |

## Sudoku Puzzle 18

| 1 | 2 | 9 | 8 | 5 | 6 | 3 | 7 | 4 |
|---|---|---|---|---|---|---|---|---|
| 4 | 7 | 5 | 2 | 3 | 9 | 8 | 6 | 1 |
| 8 | 6 | 3 | 7 | 1 | 4 | 5 | 9 | 2 |
| 5 | 8 | 2 | 3 | 7 | 1 | 9 | 4 | 6 |
| 7 | 1 | 4 | 6 | 9 | 8 | 2 | 5 | 3 |
| 9 | 3 | 6 | 4 | 2 | 5 | 1 | 8 | 7 |
| 6 | 9 | 1 | 5 | 4 | 3 | 7 | 2 | 8 |
| 3 | 4 | 7 | 9 | 8 | 2 | 6 | 1 | 5 |
| 2 | 5 | 8 | 1 | 6 | 7 | 4 | 3 | 9 |

## Sudoku Puzzle 20

| 4 | 1 | 3 | 7 | 5 | 8 | 2 | 9 | 6 |
|---|---|---|---|---|---|---|---|---|
| 2 | 7 | 8 | 6 | 4 | 9 | 3 | 1 | 5 |
| 5 | 6 | 9 | 2 | 3 | 1 | 4 | 7 | 8 |
| 3 | 9 | 6 | 1 | 7 | 2 | 5 | 8 | 4 |
| 1 | 8 | 2 | 4 | 6 | 5 | 7 | 3 | 9 |
| 7 | 4 | 5 | 9 | 8 | 3 | 6 | 2 | 1 |
| 8 | 2 | 4 | 5 | 9 | 7 | 1 | 6 | 3 |
| 9 | 5 | 1 | 3 | 2 | 6 | 8 | 4 | 7 |
| 6 | 3 | 7 | 8 | 1 | 4 | 9 | 5 | 2 |

## Sudoku Puzzle 21

| 1 | 4 | 5 | 9 | 6 | 3 | 7 | 2 | 8 |
| 2 | 8 | 7 | 1 | 5 | 4 | 3 | 6 | 9 |
| 6 | 3 | 9 | 7 | 2 | 8 | 5 | 1 | 4 |
| 9 | 5 | 6 | 4 | 3 | 2 | 1 | 8 | 7 |
| 3 | 7 | 4 | 8 | 1 | 6 | 2 | 9 | 5 |
| 8 | 1 | 2 | 5 | 7 | 9 | 4 | 3 | 6 |
| 4 | 2 | 3 | 6 | 8 | 5 | 9 | 7 | 1 |
| 5 | 6 | 1 | 3 | 9 | 7 | 8 | 4 | 2 |
| 7 | 9 | 8 | 2 | 4 | 1 | 6 | 5 | 3 |

## Sudoku Puzzle 23

| 5 | 3 | 4 | 8 | 7 | 2 | 1 | 6 | 9 |
| 6 | 8 | 9 | 1 | 3 | 4 | 2 | 5 | 7 |
| 1 | 2 | 7 | 6 | 9 | 5 | 8 | 4 | 3 |
| 7 | 5 | 6 | 3 | 8 | 1 | 9 | 2 | 4 |
| 9 | 1 | 3 | 4 | 2 | 6 | 5 | 7 | 8 |
| 8 | 4 | 2 | 7 | 5 | 9 | 3 | 1 | 6 |
| 3 | 6 | 8 | 2 | 1 | 7 | 4 | 9 | 5 |
| 2 | 7 | 5 | 9 | 4 | 8 | 6 | 3 | 1 |
| 4 | 9 | 1 | 5 | 6 | 3 | 7 | 8 | 2 |

## Sudoku Puzzle 22

| 4 | 2 | 3 | 1 | 7 | 8 | 6 | 9 | 5 |
| 8 | 6 | 1 | 3 | 9 | 5 | 7 | 2 | 4 |
| 5 | 9 | 7 | 4 | 6 | 2 | 1 | 8 | 3 |
| 6 | 8 | 4 | 5 | 2 | 3 | 9 | 1 | 7 |
| 7 | 3 | 9 | 8 | 1 | 6 | 4 | 5 | 2 |
| 1 | 5 | 2 | 7 | 4 | 9 | 8 | 3 | 6 |
| 2 | 4 | 5 | 6 | 8 | 1 | 3 | 7 | 9 |
| 3 | 1 | 6 | 9 | 5 | 7 | 2 | 4 | 8 |
| 9 | 7 | 8 | 2 | 3 | 4 | 5 | 6 | 1 |

## Sudoku Puzzle 24

| 8 | 4 | 3 | 9 | 7 | 6 | 5 | 2 | 1 |
| 5 | 6 | 7 | 2 | 8 | 1 | 4 | 9 | 3 |
| 9 | 2 | 1 | 3 | 5 | 4 | 7 | 6 | 8 |
| 4 | 1 | 8 | 5 | 2 | 9 | 3 | 7 | 6 |
| 7 | 3 | 2 | 6 | 1 | 8 | 9 | 4 | 5 |
| 6 | 5 | 9 | 7 | 4 | 3 | 1 | 8 | 2 |
| 3 | 8 | 4 | 1 | 9 | 2 | 6 | 5 | 7 |
| 2 | 7 | 6 | 4 | 3 | 5 | 8 | 1 | 9 |
| 1 | 9 | 5 | 8 | 6 | 7 | 2 | 3 | 4 |

## Sudoku Puzzle 25

| 8 | 1 | 3 | 6 | 2 | 5 | 4 | 7 | 9 |
|---|---|---|---|---|---|---|---|---|
| 5 | 6 | 4 | 9 | 7 | 8 | 3 | 2 | 1 |
| 2 | 9 | 7 | 4 | 3 | 1 | 5 | 6 | 8 |
| 4 | 5 | 6 | 1 | 9 | 2 | 8 | 3 | 7 |
| 3 | 8 | 1 | 7 | 4 | 6 | 2 | 9 | 5 |
| 7 | 2 | 9 | 5 | 8 | 3 | 1 | 4 | 6 |
| 6 | 7 | 2 | 8 | 5 | 4 | 9 | 1 | 3 |
| 9 | 3 | 5 | 2 | 1 | 7 | 6 | 8 | 4 |
| 1 | 4 | 8 | 3 | 6 | 9 | 7 | 5 | 2 |

## Sudoku Puzzle 27

| 9 | 1 | 7 | 8 | 6 | 3 | 5 | 2 | 4 |
|---|---|---|---|---|---|---|---|---|
| 5 | 8 | 4 | 2 | 1 | 9 | 3 | 6 | 7 |
| 6 | 2 | 3 | 5 | 4 | 7 | 1 | 9 | 8 |
| 3 | 4 | 9 | 1 | 7 | 2 | 6 | 8 | 5 |
| 1 | 7 | 6 | 4 | 5 | 8 | 2 | 3 | 9 |
| 8 | 5 | 2 | 9 | 3 | 6 | 4 | 7 | 1 |
| 7 | 3 | 5 | 6 | 8 | 1 | 9 | 4 | 2 |
| 4 | 9 | 8 | 3 | 2 | 5 | 7 | 1 | 6 |
| 2 | 6 | 1 | 7 | 9 | 4 | 8 | 5 | 3 |

## Sudoku Puzzle 26

| 6 | 9 | 5 | 3 | 1 | 8 | 7 | 4 | 2 |
|---|---|---|---|---|---|---|---|---|
| 4 | 7 | 8 | 2 | 6 | 9 | 5 | 3 | 1 |
| 1 | 3 | 2 | 7 | 5 | 4 | 8 | 6 | 9 |
| 2 | 4 | 7 | 9 | 8 | 1 | 6 | 5 | 3 |
| 8 | 1 | 6 | 5 | 4 | 3 | 2 | 9 | 7 |
| 3 | 5 | 9 | 6 | 2 | 7 | 1 | 8 | 4 |
| 5 | 6 | 4 | 1 | 9 | 2 | 3 | 7 | 8 |
| 9 | 2 | 3 | 8 | 7 | 5 | 4 | 1 | 6 |
| 7 | 8 | 1 | 4 | 3 | 6 | 9 | 2 | 5 |

## Sudoku Puzzle 28

| 7 | 9 | 1 | 2 | 5 | 3 | 6 | 4 | 8 |
|---|---|---|---|---|---|---|---|---|
| 4 | 6 | 2 | 8 | 7 | 9 | 1 | 5 | 3 |
| 3 | 8 | 5 | 1 | 6 | 4 | 2 | 7 | 9 |
| 5 | 7 | 6 | 4 | 9 | 2 | 8 | 3 | 1 |
| 1 | 4 | 3 | 7 | 8 | 6 | 9 | 2 | 5 |
| 9 | 2 | 8 | 3 | 1 | 5 | 4 | 6 | 7 |
| 8 | 1 | 4 | 6 | 3 | 7 | 5 | 9 | 2 |
| 6 | 3 | 9 | 5 | 2 | 8 | 7 | 1 | 4 |
| 2 | 5 | 7 | 9 | 4 | 1 | 3 | 8 | 6 |

## Sudoku Puzzle 29

| 3 | 6 | 2 | 4 | 9 | 5 | 8 | 1 | 7 |
| 8 | 4 | 5 | 7 | 6 | 1 | 3 | 9 | 2 |
| 9 | 7 | 1 | 8 | 3 | 2 | 4 | 6 | 5 |
| 2 | 9 | 7 | 1 | 5 | 8 | 6 | 4 | 3 |
| 6 | 1 | 3 | 9 | 7 | 4 | 2 | 5 | 8 |
| 4 | 5 | 8 | 3 | 2 | 6 | 1 | 7 | 9 |
| 7 | 2 | 4 | 6 | 8 | 9 | 5 | 3 | 1 |
| 1 | 8 | 9 | 5 | 4 | 3 | 7 | 2 | 6 |
| 5 | 3 | 6 | 2 | 1 | 7 | 9 | 8 | 4 |

## Sudoku Puzzle 31

| 7 | 1 | 5 | 6 | 3 | 8 | 9 | 4 | 2 |
| 8 | 9 | 3 | 4 | 2 | 5 | 7 | 1 | 6 |
| 6 | 2 | 4 | 7 | 1 | 9 | 8 | 3 | 5 |
| 9 | 8 | 6 | 1 | 5 | 4 | 3 | 2 | 7 |
| 1 | 4 | 7 | 3 | 8 | 2 | 5 | 6 | 9 |
| 3 | 5 | 2 | 9 | 6 | 7 | 4 | 8 | 1 |
| 5 | 6 | 1 | 8 | 7 | 3 | 2 | 9 | 4 |
| 4 | 7 | 8 | 2 | 9 | 6 | 1 | 5 | 3 |
| 2 | 3 | 9 | 5 | 4 | 1 | 6 | 7 | 8 |

## Sudoku Puzzle 30

| 5 | 4 | 7 | 9 | 2 | 1 | 3 | 6 | 8 |
| 9 | 8 | 1 | 7 | 6 | 3 | 4 | 2 | 5 |
| 6 | 2 | 3 | 5 | 8 | 4 | 1 | 7 | 9 |
| 8 | 5 | 9 | 1 | 4 | 6 | 7 | 3 | 2 |
| 7 | 1 | 6 | 2 | 3 | 5 | 8 | 9 | 4 |
| 4 | 3 | 2 | 8 | 9 | 7 | 6 | 5 | 1 |
| 3 | 9 | 8 | 4 | 7 | 2 | 5 | 1 | 6 |
| 2 | 6 | 5 | 3 | 1 | 8 | 9 | 4 | 7 |
| 1 | 7 | 4 | 6 | 5 | 9 | 2 | 8 | 3 |

## Sudoku Puzzle 32

| 8 | 7 | 5 | 3 | 1 | 9 | 4 | 6 | 2 |
| 6 | 3 | 9 | 4 | 2 | 5 | 7 | 8 | 1 |
| 4 | 1 | 2 | 6 | 7 | 8 | 3 | 9 | 5 |
| 3 | 5 | 8 | 1 | 6 | 2 | 9 | 7 | 4 |
| 9 | 2 | 6 | 8 | 4 | 7 | 1 | 5 | 3 |
| 1 | 4 | 7 | 5 | 9 | 3 | 8 | 2 | 6 |
| 5 | 6 | 1 | 9 | 8 | 4 | 2 | 3 | 7 |
| 7 | 9 | 3 | 2 | 5 | 1 | 6 | 4 | 8 |
| 2 | 8 | 4 | 7 | 3 | 6 | 5 | 1 | 9 |

## Sudoku Puzzle 33

| 7 | 6 | 1 | 2 | 8 | 5 | 9 | 3 | 4 |
| 5 | 3 | 2 | 9 | 4 | 7 | 1 | 8 | 6 |
| 9 | 4 | 8 | 3 | 6 | 1 | 7 | 5 | 2 |
| 4 | 9 | 7 | 6 | 2 | 8 | 5 | 1 | 3 |
| 8 | 5 | 3 | 7 | 1 | 4 | 2 | 6 | 9 |
| 1 | 2 | 6 | 5 | 9 | 3 | 4 | 7 | 8 |
| 3 | 1 | 4 | 8 | 7 | 9 | 6 | 2 | 5 |
| 6 | 8 | 9 | 1 | 5 | 2 | 3 | 4 | 7 |
| 2 | 7 | 5 | 4 | 3 | 6 | 8 | 9 | 1 |

## Sudoku Puzzle 35

| 1 | 4 | 8 | 6 | 7 | 3 | 5 | 2 | 9 |
| 3 | 7 | 5 | 2 | 4 | 9 | 1 | 8 | 6 |
| 6 | 9 | 2 | 5 | 8 | 1 | 7 | 4 | 3 |
| 9 | 1 | 7 | 4 | 5 | 8 | 3 | 6 | 2 |
| 2 | 8 | 6 | 1 | 3 | 7 | 9 | 5 | 4 |
| 5 | 3 | 4 | 9 | 6 | 2 | 8 | 7 | 1 |
| 4 | 2 | 3 | 8 | 1 | 5 | 6 | 9 | 7 |
| 7 | 5 | 9 | 3 | 2 | 6 | 4 | 1 | 8 |
| 8 | 6 | 1 | 7 | 9 | 4 | 2 | 3 | 5 |

## Sudoku Puzzle 34

| 5 | 9 | 1 | 2 | 3 | 7 | 4 | 8 | 6 |
| 4 | 3 | 8 | 5 | 9 | 6 | 1 | 2 | 7 |
| 7 | 2 | 6 | 8 | 1 | 4 | 3 | 9 | 5 |
| 9 | 4 | 5 | 7 | 2 | 3 | 8 | 6 | 1 |
| 1 | 6 | 7 | 9 | 5 | 8 | 2 | 3 | 4 |
| 2 | 8 | 3 | 6 | 4 | 1 | 5 | 7 | 9 |
| 6 | 5 | 4 | 3 | 8 | 9 | 7 | 1 | 2 |
| 3 | 1 | 9 | 4 | 7 | 2 | 6 | 5 | 8 |
| 8 | 7 | 2 | 1 | 6 | 5 | 9 | 4 | 3 |

## Sudoku Puzzle 36

| 1 | 6 | 9 | 3 | 7 | 5 | 2 | 4 | 8 |
| 7 | 4 | 8 | 9 | 1 | 2 | 6 | 3 | 5 |
| 5 | 2 | 3 | 6 | 4 | 8 | 9 | 7 | 1 |
| 4 | 8 | 7 | 5 | 9 | 1 | 3 | 6 | 2 |
| 3 | 9 | 5 | 2 | 6 | 7 | 8 | 1 | 4 |
| 6 | 1 | 2 | 4 | 8 | 3 | 7 | 5 | 9 |
| 9 | 7 | 4 | 1 | 2 | 6 | 5 | 8 | 3 |
| 8 | 5 | 1 | 7 | 3 | 9 | 4 | 2 | 6 |
| 2 | 3 | 6 | 8 | 5 | 4 | 1 | 9 | 7 |

## Sudoku Puzzle 37

| 1 | 6 | 2 | 8 | 5 | 4 | 9 | 3 | 7 |
|---|---|---|---|---|---|---|---|---|
| 5 | 3 | 9 | 7 | 6 | 2 | 8 | 4 | 1 |
| 7 | 4 | 8 | 1 | 9 | 3 | 5 | 2 | 6 |
| 6 | 2 | 3 | 4 | 7 | 8 | 1 | 9 | 5 |
| 8 | 7 | 1 | 5 | 2 | 9 | 3 | 6 | 4 |
| 9 | 5 | 4 | 6 | 3 | 1 | 7 | 8 | 2 |
| 4 | 9 | 7 | 2 | 8 | 5 | 6 | 1 | 3 |
| 3 | 1 | 6 | 9 | 4 | 7 | 2 | 5 | 8 |
| 2 | 8 | 5 | 3 | 1 | 6 | 4 | 7 | 9 |

## Sudoku Puzzle 39

| 4 | 8 | 6 | 5 | 9 | 3 | 1 | 7 | 2 |
|---|---|---|---|---|---|---|---|---|
| 5 | 7 | 2 | 4 | 8 | 1 | 3 | 9 | 6 |
| 3 | 1 | 9 | 7 | 6 | 2 | 8 | 5 | 4 |
| 7 | 4 | 3 | 9 | 1 | 6 | 5 | 2 | 8 |
| 2 | 6 | 8 | 3 | 5 | 4 | 7 | 1 | 9 |
| 1 | 9 | 5 | 8 | 2 | 7 | 4 | 6 | 3 |
| 9 | 2 | 7 | 1 | 4 | 8 | 6 | 3 | 5 |
| 6 | 3 | 4 | 2 | 7 | 5 | 9 | 8 | 1 |
| 8 | 5 | 1 | 6 | 3 | 9 | 2 | 4 | 7 |

## Sudoku Puzzle 38

| 9 | 2 | 6 | 7 | 8 | 4 | 1 | 5 | 3 |
|---|---|---|---|---|---|---|---|---|
| 8 | 1 | 7 | 5 | 3 | 6 | 9 | 4 | 2 |
| 5 | 4 | 3 | 1 | 2 | 9 | 8 | 7 | 6 |
| 7 | 6 | 4 | 9 | 5 | 8 | 2 | 3 | 1 |
| 2 | 9 | 5 | 3 | 1 | 7 | 6 | 8 | 4 |
| 3 | 8 | 1 | 4 | 6 | 2 | 5 | 9 | 7 |
| 4 | 3 | 8 | 6 | 9 | 1 | 7 | 2 | 5 |
| 6 | 7 | 9 | 2 | 4 | 5 | 3 | 1 | 8 |
| 1 | 5 | 2 | 8 | 7 | 3 | 4 | 6 | 9 |

## Sudoku Puzzle 40

| 6 | 2 | 8 | 7 | 1 | 3 | 5 | 9 | 4 |
|---|---|---|---|---|---|---|---|---|
| 1 | 3 | 9 | 5 | 2 | 4 | 6 | 7 | 8 |
| 7 | 4 | 5 | 8 | 6 | 9 | 3 | 2 | 1 |
| 8 | 9 | 6 | 4 | 3 | 7 | 1 | 5 | 2 |
| 2 | 5 | 3 | 1 | 8 | 6 | 9 | 4 | 7 |
| 4 | 1 | 7 | 9 | 5 | 2 | 8 | 3 | 6 |
| 5 | 7 | 2 | 6 | 9 | 1 | 4 | 8 | 3 |
| 9 | 6 | 4 | 3 | 7 | 8 | 2 | 1 | 5 |
| 3 | 8 | 1 | 2 | 4 | 5 | 7 | 6 | 9 |

## Sudoku Puzzle 41

| 6 | 2 | 7 | 8 | 3 | 9 | 1 | 5 | 4 |
|---|---|---|---|---|---|---|---|---|
| 5 | 4 | 8 | 2 | 6 | 1 | 9 | 3 | 7 |
| 9 | 1 | 3 | 7 | 5 | 4 | 8 | 6 | 2 |
| 4 | 9 | 2 | 3 | 8 | 5 | 6 | 7 | 1 |
| 1 | 7 | 5 | 4 | 2 | 6 | 3 | 8 | 9 |
| 8 | 3 | 6 | 9 | 1 | 7 | 4 | 2 | 5 |
| 3 | 8 | 9 | 1 | 7 | 2 | 5 | 4 | 6 |
| 2 | 5 | 1 | 6 | 4 | 8 | 7 | 9 | 3 |
| 7 | 6 | 4 | 5 | 9 | 3 | 2 | 1 | 8 |

## Sudoku Puzzle 43

| 4 | 6 | 3 | 7 | 9 | 5 | 2 | 1 | 8 |
|---|---|---|---|---|---|---|---|---|
| 5 | 9 | 8 | 2 | 1 | 6 | 7 | 4 | 3 |
| 7 | 2 | 1 | 3 | 4 | 8 | 5 | 9 | 6 |
| 2 | 5 | 9 | 4 | 8 | 3 | 6 | 7 | 1 |
| 8 | 4 | 7 | 6 | 5 | 1 | 3 | 2 | 9 |
| 1 | 3 | 6 | 9 | 7 | 2 | 8 | 5 | 4 |
| 6 | 8 | 4 | 5 | 2 | 9 | 1 | 3 | 7 |
| 9 | 1 | 2 | 8 | 3 | 7 | 4 | 6 | 5 |
| 3 | 7 | 5 | 1 | 6 | 4 | 9 | 8 | 2 |

## Sudoku Puzzle 42

| 1 | 7 | 3 | 6 | 4 | 8 | 5 | 2 | 9 |
|---|---|---|---|---|---|---|---|---|
| 4 | 5 | 8 | 1 | 9 | 2 | 3 | 6 | 7 |
| 6 | 2 | 9 | 5 | 7 | 3 | 8 | 4 | 1 |
| 8 | 9 | 1 | 4 | 6 | 5 | 2 | 7 | 3 |
| 2 | 4 | 5 | 8 | 3 | 7 | 1 | 9 | 6 |
| 7 | 3 | 6 | 2 | 1 | 9 | 4 | 5 | 8 |
| 5 | 8 | 7 | 9 | 2 | 1 | 6 | 3 | 4 |
| 9 | 6 | 2 | 3 | 8 | 4 | 7 | 1 | 5 |
| 3 | 1 | 4 | 7 | 5 | 6 | 9 | 8 | 2 |

## Sudoku Puzzle 44

| 5 | 8 | 9 | 3 | 2 | 7 | 6 | 4 | 1 |
|---|---|---|---|---|---|---|---|---|
| 7 | 2 | 1 | 6 | 5 | 4 | 3 | 9 | 8 |
| 6 | 4 | 3 | 1 | 9 | 8 | 2 | 5 | 7 |
| 9 | 3 | 4 | 8 | 1 | 6 | 7 | 2 | 5 |
| 1 | 5 | 8 | 7 | 4 | 2 | 9 | 6 | 3 |
| 2 | 6 | 7 | 5 | 3 | 9 | 1 | 8 | 4 |
| 3 | 1 | 6 | 9 | 8 | 5 | 4 | 7 | 2 |
| 8 | 7 | 2 | 4 | 6 | 3 | 5 | 1 | 9 |
| 4 | 9 | 5 | 2 | 7 | 1 | 8 | 3 | 6 |

## Sudoku Puzzle 45

| 3 | 6 | 1 | 2 | 7 | 8 | 9 | 4 | 5 |
|---|---|---|---|---|---|---|---|---|
| 7 | 4 | 9 | 1 | 6 | 5 | 2 | 3 | 8 |
| 2 | 8 | 5 | 3 | 4 | 9 | 7 | 1 | 6 |
| 6 | 2 | 4 | 9 | 8 | 7 | 1 | 5 | 3 |
| 1 | 5 | 3 | 6 | 2 | 4 | 8 | 9 | 7 |
| 9 | 7 | 8 | 5 | 3 | 1 | 6 | 2 | 4 |
| 8 | 9 | 7 | 4 | 5 | 2 | 3 | 6 | 1 |
| 5 | 1 | 6 | 7 | 9 | 3 | 4 | 8 | 2 |
| 4 | 3 | 2 | 8 | 1 | 6 | 5 | 7 | 9 |

## Sudoku Puzzle 47

| 5 | 9 | 3 | 8 | 1 | 2 | 4 | 6 | 7 |
|---|---|---|---|---|---|---|---|---|
| 2 | 6 | 4 | 7 | 3 | 5 | 1 | 8 | 9 |
| 1 | 8 | 7 | 4 | 9 | 6 | 3 | 5 | 2 |
| 9 | 3 | 6 | 5 | 2 | 1 | 7 | 4 | 8 |
| 4 | 7 | 5 | 3 | 6 | 8 | 2 | 9 | 1 |
| 8 | 2 | 1 | 9 | 7 | 4 | 6 | 3 | 5 |
| 6 | 4 | 2 | 1 | 5 | 9 | 8 | 7 | 3 |
| 7 | 1 | 9 | 6 | 8 | 3 | 5 | 2 | 4 |
| 3 | 5 | 8 | 2 | 4 | 7 | 9 | 1 | 6 |

## Sudoku Puzzle 46

| 5 | 2 | 1 | 9 | 8 | 7 | 6 | 3 | 4 |
|---|---|---|---|---|---|---|---|---|
| 9 | 7 | 3 | 6 | 4 | 5 | 8 | 1 | 2 |
| 8 | 6 | 4 | 3 | 2 | 1 | 7 | 9 | 5 |
| 4 | 1 | 7 | 5 | 3 | 2 | 9 | 6 | 8 |
| 2 | 3 | 9 | 8 | 1 | 6 | 4 | 5 | 7 |
| 6 | 8 | 5 | 4 | 7 | 9 | 1 | 2 | 3 |
| 7 | 4 | 2 | 1 | 6 | 3 | 5 | 8 | 9 |
| 3 | 9 | 6 | 7 | 5 | 8 | 2 | 4 | 1 |
| 1 | 5 | 8 | 2 | 9 | 4 | 3 | 7 | 6 |

## Sudoku Puzzle 48

| 9 | 3 | 2 | 1 | 7 | 6 | 8 | 4 | 5 |
|---|---|---|---|---|---|---|---|---|
| 5 | 1 | 4 | 3 | 2 | 8 | 9 | 7 | 6 |
| 7 | 8 | 6 | 4 | 9 | 5 | 2 | 3 | 1 |
| 3 | 7 | 5 | 6 | 8 | 1 | 4 | 9 | 2 |
| 2 | 4 | 8 | 9 | 5 | 7 | 1 | 6 | 3 |
| 6 | 9 | 1 | 2 | 4 | 3 | 7 | 5 | 8 |
| 8 | 6 | 7 | 5 | 1 | 4 | 3 | 2 | 9 |
| 4 | 5 | 9 | 8 | 3 | 2 | 6 | 1 | 7 |
| 1 | 2 | 3 | 7 | 6 | 9 | 5 | 8 | 4 |

## Sudoku Puzzle 49

| 4 | 6 | 8 | 7 | 2 | 3 | 5 | 9 | 1 |
| 7 | 5 | 3 | 9 | 8 | 1 | 4 | 2 | 6 |
| 2 | 9 | 1 | 6 | 5 | 4 | 8 | 3 | 7 |
| 1 | 7 | 5 | 2 | 6 | 8 | 3 | 4 | 9 |
| 3 | 2 | 4 | 1 | 9 | 5 | 7 | 6 | 8 |
| 6 | 8 | 9 | 3 | 4 | 7 | 1 | 5 | 2 |
| 8 | 4 | 6 | 5 | 7 | 2 | 9 | 1 | 3 |
| 5 | 1 | 2 | 8 | 3 | 9 | 6 | 7 | 4 |
| 9 | 3 | 7 | 4 | 1 | 6 | 2 | 8 | 5 |

## Sudoku Puzzle 50

| 9 | 3 | 2 | 4 | 5 | 1 | 8 | 6 | 7 |
| 4 | 5 | 1 | 6 | 7 | 8 | 9 | 2 | 3 |
| 8 | 7 | 6 | 3 | 9 | 2 | 5 | 1 | 4 |
| 6 | 4 | 9 | 7 | 8 | 5 | 2 | 3 | 1 |
| 3 | 2 | 8 | 1 | 6 | 4 | 7 | 9 | 5 |
| 5 | 1 | 7 | 9 | 2 | 3 | 4 | 8 | 6 |
| 2 | 9 | 4 | 5 | 1 | 6 | 3 | 7 | 8 |
| 7 | 6 | 5 | 8 | 3 | 9 | 1 | 4 | 2 |
| 1 | 8 | 3 | 2 | 4 | 7 | 6 | 5 | 9 |

# Logic Puzzle Answers

## Card Logic Puzzle 1: C

The last three cards in Row B are the same cards as the first three in Row A, but in reverse order. This suggests that the rows are in reverse order. So the missing fourth card in Row A is the first one in Row B—the eight of spades. Just for the sake of completeness, note that in Row A each card is twice the one to its left; in Row B, which is the reverse of Row A, each card is half the one to its left (of course). Also, all four suits are used.

## Card Logic Puzzle 2: D

Each hand has an ace, a three, a four, and a five—but of different suits (of course). Missing from Hand 3 is the four of diamonds. Note that the four of hearts is already used in Hand 1.

## Card Logic Puzzle 3: D

Each hand has the four suits—a heart, a club, a spade, and a diamond. The value of the cards is not relevant. Missing from the fourth hand is a spade since it has the other three suits.

## Card Logic Puzzle 4: A

There are two parts to the solution. (1) Only the black symbols (spades and clubs) are found in the odd-numbered columns (columns 1, 3, 5), and only the red symbols (hearts and diamonds) are found in the even-numbered columns

(columns 2, 4, 6). (2) In each column, the two symbols are alternated; that is, a spade is immediately above or below a club, and a heart is immediately above or below a diamond. So according to this two-part placement system, a heart is missing from the second cell of the second column.

## Card Logic Puzzle 5: C

For each hand, add the number values of the top two cards and you will get the third card down from the top. The fourth or bottom card is a distracter—that is, it is irrelevant to the solution.

## Card Logic Puzzle 6: B

For each hand, the number values of the top two cards and the number values of the bottom two cards, when added together, produce the same total. Here are the totals produced by adding the cards in each column according to this pattern:

**Hand 1:** total of 5 (3 + 2 = 4 + 1)
**Hand 2:** total of 8 (5 + 3 = 2 + 6)
**Hand 3:** total of 6 (4 + 2 = 1 + 5)
**Hand 4:** total of 10 (1 + 9 = 8 + 2)

If you look at the grid horizontally instead of vertically, you'll see that D could also work as an answer. How? The numerical value of each row decreases by one. Here are the totals:

**Row 1:** total of 17 (7 + 5 + 4 + 1)
**Row 2:** total of 16 (2 + 3 + 2 + 9)
**Row 3:** total of 15 (4 + 2 + 1 + 8)
**Row 4:** total of 14 (1 + 6 + 5 + 2)

## Card Logic Puzzle 7: A

For this puzzle, you will have to look in both directions—vertically (columns) and horizontally (rows). First, each column has cards of the same suit (all spades, all hearts, all clubs, all diamonds). Second, in each row the number value of the last card to the right is the sum of the values of the previous three cards.

## Domino Logic Puzzle 1: Tile 5

The number of spots in the bottom part of each tile is one more than the number of spots in the top part. The exception is Tile 5.

## Domino Logic Puzzle 2: Tile 6

Here's the rule: The number of top and bottom spots in each successive tile increases by one. If you look at only the top spots in each tile, you will see this sequence:

**Tile 1:** one spot

**Tile 2:** two spots

**Tile 3:** three spots

**Tile 4:** four spots

**Tile 5:** five spots

The same rule applies to the bottom spots. Note that these start at two spots.

**Tile 1:** two spots

**Tile 2:** three spots

**Tile 3:** four spots

**Tile 4:** five spots

**Tile 5:** six spots

Clearly, Tile 6 does not belong.

## Domino Logic Puzzle 3: Column 4

The total number of spots in the two tiles of a column is the same. The exception, as you can see, is Column 4:

**Column 1:**

**Tile 1:** $1 + 4 = 5$

**Tile 2:** $2 + 3 = 5$

**Column 2:**

**Tile 1:** $2 + 4 = 6$

**Tile 2:** $1 + 5 = 6$

**Column 3:**

**Tile 1:** $3 + 5 = 8$

**Tile 2:** $4 + 4 = 8$

**Column 4:**

**Tile 1:** $1 + 6 = 7$

**Tile 2:** $4 + 5 = 9$

## Domino Logic Puzzle 4: Tile 4

The spots on each tile, when added together, produce an even number. For example, in Tile 1, the total number of spots is ten ($4 + 6 = 10$), an even number. The exception is Tile 4, in which the number of spots adds up to an odd number, five ($2 + 3 = 5$).

## Domino Logic Puzzle 5: Tile 5

Domino Logic Puzzle 4 involved even numbers; this one involves odd numbers instead. The spots on each tile when added together produce an odd number. The exception is Tile 5, in which the number of spots adds up to an even number.

## Domino Logic Puzzle 6: Column 4

Each fraction at the bottom of a column is constructed as follows: (1) the numerator consists of the sum of all the spots in the top parts of each tile in a column; (2) the denominator consists of the sum of all the spots in the bottom parts of each tile in a column. Let's do Column 1 for the sake of illustration. Tile 1 refers to the top tile, Tile 2 to the one below it, and so on.

**Top part of Tile 1:** two spots
**Top part of Tile 2:** three spots
**Top part of Tile 3:** one spot
**Top part of Tile 4:** one spot
**Total:** 2 + 3 + 1 + 1 = 7

This number is the numerator of the fraction given at the bottom.

**Bottom part of Tile 1:** four spots
**Bottom part of Tile 2:** four spots
**Bottom part of Tile 3:** two spots
**Bottom part of Tile 4:** three spots
**Total:** 4 + 4 + 2 + 3 = 13

This number is the denominator of the fraction given at the bottom. The fraction is 7/13. The column that breaks this pattern is the fourth one, as you can check for yourself. The fraction at the bottom should be 10/20, not 11/20.

## Domino Logic Puzzle 7: Column 3

This is a tricky one. Each number at the bottom of the column is produced as follows: (1) subtract the top spot(s) from the bottom spot(s) in each tile in the column; (2) add all the results together; (3) this produces the number at the bottom of the column. Let's do Column 1 for the sake of illustration. Tile 1 refers to the top tile, Tile 2 to the one below it, and so on.

**Tile 1:**
**Top part:** two spots
**Bottom part:** six spots
**Bottom − Top:** 6 − 2 = 4

**Tile 3:**
**Top part:** two spots
**Bottom part:** four spots
**Bottom − Top:** 4 − 2 = 2

**Tile 2:**
**Top part:** three spots
**Bottom part:** five spots
**Bottom − Top:** 5 − 3 = 2

**Tile 4:**
**Top part:** one spot
**Bottom part:** four spots
**Bottom − Top:** 4 − 1 = 3

**Total of all the differences:** 4 + 2 + 2 + 3 = 11

This number is the one given at the bottom. The column that breaks this pattern is the third one. For Column 3, totaling the differences gives you: 3 + 1 + 1 + 2 = 7, not 5.

## Lie Detection Puzzle 1: Alina

All the statements were true. So the ones who say they are innocent are indeed innocent. These are Andy, Art, Alexa, and Ariana. Who does this leave? Alina. She also told the truth—Alexa, as she says, is indeed innocent. But this changes nothing. Alina is our culprit.

## Lie Detection Puzzle 2: Brent

All the statements were false. So the person accused in a statement is, contrarily, innocent. Let's go through who the accused ones are: Ben (accused by Bob), Barb (accused by Brent), Bob (accused by Bertha), and Bertha (accused by Ben). So these four are, contrarily, all innocent. Who does this leave? Brent. So he's our robber. Incidentally, Barb's statement, "I don't know who did it," changes nothing. It is simply false according to what we are told.

## Lie Detection Puzzle 3: Chuck

The statements made by Cam and Charlotte indicate the same thing—namely, that Cam is innocent. So they are logically both true or both false. They cannot be both false because there was only one false statement in the set. So they are both true. Similarly, the statements made by Carroll and Claudia indicate the same thing—namely, that Carroll is innocent. Again, they must be both true or both false. They cannot be both false because there was only one false statement in the set. So they are both true. We have now identified the four true statements. This leaves Chuck's statement as the only false one. So, contrary to what he says, Chuck is our culprit since we are told that the embezzler was also the only liar.

## Lie Detection Puzzle 4: Eric

The statements made by Evan, Elana, and Emma indicate the same thing—namely, that Elvira is the killer. So they are logically all true or all false. They cannot be true because there were only two, not three, true statements in the set. So they are all false. This means two things: (a) Elvira is not the killer, contrary to what they say; (b) the statements by Eric and Elvira were the two true ones. So Eric or Elvira is the killer, since we are told that the killer was one of the two who told the truth. We have already deduced that Elvira is not the killer. So it is Eric. By the way, both Eric and Elvira truthfully state that Evan lied—as we know. But this changes nothing. We have our killer.

## Lie Detection Puzzle 5: Frank

The statement made by Frank and the one made by Felicia contradict each other—Felicia says she is innocent, while Frank points the finger at her. So one is true and the other false. Similarly, the statement made by Fanny and the one made by Faustus contradict each other—Faustus says he is innocent, while Fanny points the finger at him. So one is true and the other false. In these four statements, considered together, there are, therefore, two true and two false statements—we're not sure which is which, for now. What this means, though, is that the third missing truthful statement belongs to Filomena. She fingers Frank, and, being a truthful statement, we now have our robber. You can now identify the other truth tellers and the liars on your own if you so wish.

## Lie Detection Puzzle 6: Gabby

The statement made by Grant and the one made by Gail contradict each other—Grant says he is innocent, while Gail points the finger at him. So one is true and the other false. Similarly, the statement made by Glenda and the one made by Gaston contradict each other—Glenda says she is innocent, while Gaston points the finger at her. So one is true and the other false. In these four statements, considered together, there are, therefore, two true and two false statements—as above, we're not sure which is which for now. What this means, though, is that the third missing false statement belongs to Gabby. Despite her declaration of innocence, we now have our killer. You can now identify the other truth tellers and the liars on your own if you wish.

## Lie Detection Puzzle 7: Hank

The statements made by Hank, Helen, and Hubert indicate the same thing—namely, that Hank is innocent. So they are logically all true or all false. They cannot be true because there were only two, not three, true statements in the set. So they are all false. This means we have identified our killer—it's Hank. His claim of innocence is false, and he is thus our killer. The remaining two statements by Harry and Hanna are the two true ones. Both truthfully claim innocence.

## Lie Detection Puzzle 8: Ivan

Inez and Irene say the same thing—namely, that Inez is innocent. Iris and Ivan contradict this, saying that Inez is guilty. In these four statements, considered together, there are two true and two false statements—we're not sure which is which for now. The third false statement in the set was made by Ida. She says that Ivan is innocent. This is a false statement, so, contrary to what Ida says, Ivan is our culprit.

## Lie Detection Puzzle 9: Jack

The statements made by Jack, Jane, and Jill indicate the same thing—namely, that Jane is innocent. They are logically all true or all false. They cannot be false because there were only two false statements in the set. So they are all true, and thus, Jane is innocent. This means that one of the other two is the guilty hacker since, as we are told, the guilty hacker was one of the truth tellers. It also means that the statements by Jim and Jenna are the two false ones. Let's consider each one. Jim says, "Jane did it." As we now know, this is patently false, but it does not help us much. Consider Jenna's statement, "Jack is innocent." As we know, this is also a false statement. So, contrary to what Jenna says, Jack is our guilty hacker. As expected, he was a truth teller.

## Lie Detection Puzzle 10: Kayla

The statements made by Kyle and Kayla contradict each other—Kyle says he is innocent, while Kayla points the finger at him. So one is true and the other false. Similarly, the statements made by Karen and Ken contradict each other—Karen says she is innocent, while Ken points the finger at her. So one is true and the other false. In these four statements, considered together, there are, therefore, two true and two false statements—as in previous puzzles, we're not sure which is which for now. What this means, though, is that the third missing false statement belongs to Kristina. She says that Kayla is innocent. But we know this is false. So, contrary to what she says, Kayla is our murderer. You can determine the truthfulness or falsity of the other statements yourself if you so wish.

## Lie Detection Puzzle 11: Louise

All the statements were true. So the people who are indicated as innocent are indeed innocent. Who are they? They are Laura (statements 1 and 10), Lisa (statements 2 and 9), Lenny (statements 3 and 8), and Linda (statements 4 and 7). Who does this leave? Louise. Her two statements (5 and 6) change nothing. She simply says, truthfully, that Laura and Linda told the truth. She is still our killer.

## Lie Detection Puzzle 12: Sandra

Samuel's statement (5) is true—as we are told as well. Since each individual made a true and a false statement, his second statement (6) is his false one. It says that Shane is the robber. So, contrary to what it says, Shane is not the robber, and we can eliminate him from the list of suspects. We can also see that Shane's statement (1) is true. Which means his statement (2) is false, eliminating Steve. Steve's statement (7) is true—as we are told there were indeed five false statements in the set. This means his second statement (8) is his false one. It says that Sheila is the robber. So, contrary to what it says, Sheila is not the robber, and we can eliminate her from the list of suspects. We can also see that Sheila's statement (3) is true, as is Sandra's statement (9). What have we got so far? Well, we have identified the five true statements—1, 3, 5, 7, and 9. The false ones are 2, 4, 6, 8, and 10. Look at statement 10. Sandra says she didn't do it. But we now know this is false. So, contrary to what she says, she's our culprit.

## Geometric Figure Puzzle 1: A

The square stands for 1.

The pentagon stands for 5.

The triangle stands for 3.

$1 + 5 + 3 = 9$

$1 + 1 + 1 + 1 = 4$

$5 - 3 = 2$

$5 + 5 \text{ (missing)} - 3 = 7$

## Geometric Figure Puzzle 2: B

The pentagon stands for 4. $\quad 4 \times 5 - 3 = 17$

The triangle stands for 5. $\quad 3 \times 3 = 9$

The circle stands for 3. $\quad 4 \times 4 = 16$

$4 + 3 + 3 \text{ (missing)} = 10$

## Geometric Figure Puzzle 3: C

The square stands for 7. $\quad 7 + 7 + 1 + 1 = 16$

The circle stands for 1. $\quad 7 + 7 + 1 = 15$

The triangle stands for 3. $\quad 3 + 1 + 1 + 1 = 6$

$7 + 1 + 3 + 7 \text{ (missing)} = 18$

## Geometric Figure Puzzle 4: D

The circle stands for 2. $\quad 2 + 3 + 1 + 5 = 11$

The triangle stands for 3. $\quad 1 \times 5 \times 1 = 5$

The square stands for 1. $\quad 3 + 3 + 3 = 9$

The hexagon stands for 5. $\quad 2 + 1 + 1 + 5 \text{ (missing)} = 9$

## Geometric Figure Puzzle 5: D

The cube stands for 3. $\quad 3 \times 2 = 6$

The cylinder stands for 2. $\quad 1 + 2 = 3$

The parallelogram stands for 1. $\quad 1 \times 2 = 2$

The diamond stands for 5. $\quad 3 \times 5 = 15$

$3 + 2 + 5 = 10 \text{ (missing)}$

## Geometric Figure Puzzle 6: A

| | |
|---|---|
| The pentagon stands for 4. | $4 \times 2 = 8$ |
| The square stands for 2. | $3 \times 1 = 3$ |
| The cube stands for 3. | $4 \times 3 = 12$ |
| The circle stands for 1. | $2 \times 1 = 2$ |
| | $4 + 2 + 3 + 1 = 10$ (missing) |

## Geometric Figure Puzzle 7: C

| | |
|---|---|
| The cube stands for 5. | $5 \times 3 = 15$ |
| The square stands for 3. | $3 + 2 = 5$ |
| The circle stands for 2. | $2 \times 5 = 10$ |
| The pentagon stands for 1. | $3 - 1 = 2$ |
| | $5 + 3 + 1 + 2 = 11$ (missing) |

## Box Puzzle 1

**A:** 2 blue   **B:** 1 red   **C:** 2 red

Since someone drew a blue ball from Box A, we can now be sure that it contains the two blue balls. There are now only red balls left (one red or two red). B's label says it contains two red, but this is false. So it contains one red ball, and this leaves the two red for C.

## Box Puzzle 2

**A:** 3 blue   **B:** 3 green   **C:** 1 red, 1 blue, 1 green

Since Box A is labeled incorrectly, we know it does not contain one red, one blue, and one green. So it contains either three blue balls or three green balls. Since a blue ball was drawn from A, it means that it contains three blue ones. We know that Box C does not contain three green balls because of the wrong label, and it does not contain three blue balls (A does). So by elimination, it contains one red, one blue, and one green ball. This means that Box B contains the remaining three green balls.

## Box Puzzle 3

**A:** 1 red   **B:** 5 red, 5 blue, 5 green   **C:** zero balls

If someone draws a green ball from any box, it means that it will contain the five red, five blue, and five green balls, since the other two boxes do not contain any green balls. Since a green ball was drawn from Box B, it means that it is the one with the five red, five blue, and five green balls. We know that Box C does not contain the one red ball because of the mislabeling, and it's not the box with the five red, five blue, and five green balls (B is). So it contains zero balls. This means that Box A contains the remaining red ball.

## Box Puzzle 4

**A:** 2 green, 1 red   **B:** 5 red   **C:** 1 blue

Drawing more than one red ball from any box means that it will contain the five red balls since there is only a single red ball in one of the other boxes. This means that the five red balls are in B, from which three red balls were drawn. Box C does not contain the two green balls and one red ball, because it is mislabeled. So it contains one blue ball, and by elimination A contains two green balls and one red ball.

## Box Puzzle 5

**A:** 1 red, 1 white   **B:** 1 green, 1 white   **C:** 9 red, 1 white

Drawing more than one red ball from any box means that it will contain the nine red balls, since there is only a single red ball in one of the other boxes. This means that the set of nine red balls and the one white one is in C, from which two red balls were drawn. B's label says that it contains one red and one white, but this is wrong because of the incorrect label, and it does not contain the nine red and one white (C does). So it contains one green and one white. This leaves one red and one white in A.

## Box Puzzle 6

**A:** 2 red, 3 white   **B:** 2 green   **C:** 2 white, 1 red

Consider Box B. It has just two balls within it. Since the only color of the balls is green (as indicated), we can conclude that the color of both balls is green. The red and white balls are distributed in Boxes A and C, adding up to eight balls in total as can be seen from the top labels. We are told that there are three white balls in one of the boxes. That box cannot be C, because it has three in total and at least one of these has to be red. So Box A is the one with three white balls, meaning that its two remaining balls are red. The other two white balls are in C, which has three balls in total, meaning that it has one red ball.

## Box Puzzle 7

**A:** 1 blue, 1 red, 2 green, 1 white   **B:** 1 blue, 2 red
**C:** 1 blue, 2 white

There are three blue balls in total, and so we can easily see from the color contents of the three boxes that each one has a single blue ball in it. Consider Box B. It has three balls in it, colored blue and red. We have just discovered that it has one blue ball. So the other two balls must be red. We are told that there are three red balls in total. So the other one is in Box A. Now consider Box C. We know it has one blue ball inside. We can now deduce that the other two are colored white.

Now consider Box A. It has four colors in it. We have discovered that there is one blue and one red in it. We are told that there are three white balls overall, and two of them are in C. So the remaining white ball is in A. We have now figured out that there is one blue, one red, and one white ball in A. The remaining two balls are, therefore, green ones—remember that A has five balls in total.

# Figure-Counting Puzzle 1: 22

|   |   |
|---|---|
| 1 | |
| 2 | 3 |
| 4 | 5 6 / 7 8 |

1. 1
2. 1 + 2 + 3
3. 1 + 2 + 3 + 4 + 5 + 6 + 7 + 8
4. 2
5. 2 + 3
6. 2 + 3 + 4 + 5 + 6 + 7 + 8
7. 2 + 4
8. 3
9. 3 + 5 + 6
10. 3 + 5 + 6 + 7 + 8
11. 4
12. 4 + 5 + 7
13. 4 + 5 + 6 + 7 + 8
14. 5
15. 5 + 6
16. 5 + 6 + 7 + 8
17. 5 + 7
18. 6
19. 6 + 8
20. 7
21. 7 + 8
22. 8

# Figure-Counting Puzzle 2: 16

1. 1
2. 1 + 2 + 3 + 5
3. 1 + 5
4. 1 + 5 + 6 + 7
5. 2
6. 2 + 3
7. 2 + 3 + 4 + 8
8. 3
9. 4
10. 4 + 6 + 7 + 8
11. 4 + 8
12. 5
13. 6
14. 6 + 7
15. 7
16. 8

# Figure-Counting Puzzle 3: 35 triangles

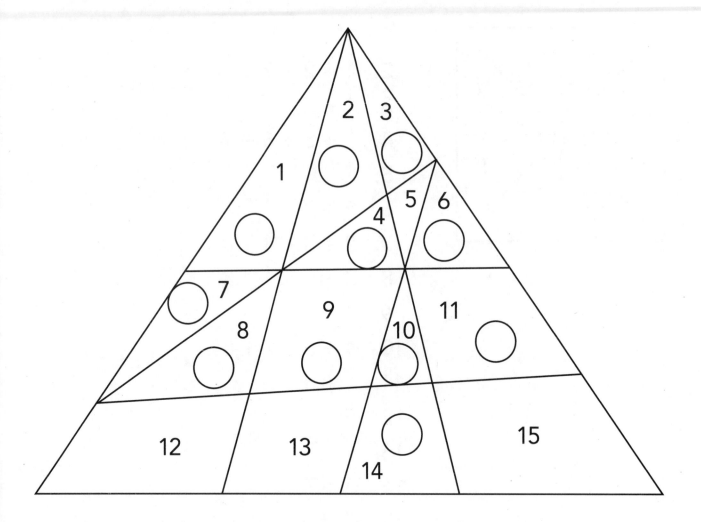

Triangle 5 is empty. Segments 9, 11, 12, 13, 14, and 15 are not triangles in themselves but may be part of assembled ones. Always remember that a circle can be contained by more than one triangle.

1. Triangle 1: one circle
2. Triangle 1 + 2 + 3 + 4 + 5 + 6: five circles
3. Triangle 1 + 2 + 3 + 4 + 5 + 6 + 7 + 8 + 9 + 10 + 11: ten circles

4. Triangle 1 + 2 + 3 + 4 + 5 + 6 + 7 + 8 + 9 + 10 + 11 + 12 + 13 + 14 + 15: eleven circles
5. Triangle 1 + 2 + 4: three circles
6. Triangle 1 + 2 + 4 + 7 + 8 + 9 + 10: seven circles
7. Triangle 1 + 2 + 4 + 7 + 8 + 9 + 10 + 12 + 13 + 14: eight circles
8. Triangle 1 + 2 + 7: three circles
9. Triangle 1 + 2 + 3 + 7: four circles
10. Triangle 2: one circle
11. Triangle 2 + 3: two circles
12. Triangle 2 + 3 + 4 + 5 + 6: four circles
13. Triangle 2 + 3 + 4 + 5 + 6 + 9 + 10 + 11: seven circles
14. Triangle 2 + 3 + 4 + 5 + 6 + 9 + 10 + 11 + 13 + 14 + 15: eight circles
15. Triangle 2 + 4: two circles
16. Triangle 2 + 4 + 9 + 10: four circles
17. Triangle 2 + 4 + 9 + 10 + 13 + 14: five circles
18. Triangle 3: one circle
19. Triangle 3 + 5: one circle
20. Triangle 3 + 5 + 6: two circles
21. Triangle 3 + 5 + 6 + 11: three circles
22. Triangle 3 + 5 + 6 + 11 + 15: three circles
23. Triangle 4: one circle
24. Triangle 4 + 5: one circle
25. Triangle 4 + 5 + 6: two circles
26. Triangle 4 + 5 + 8 + 9: three circles

27. Triangle 4 + 5 + 6 + 8 + 9 + 10 + 11: six circles
28. Triangle 4 + 8 + 9 + 10: four circles
29. Triangle 6: one circle
30. Triangle 6 + 10 + 11: three circles
31. Triangle 6 + 10 + 11 + 14 + 15: four circles
32. Triangle 7: one circle
33. Triangle 8: one circle
34. Triangle 10: one circle
35. Triangle 10 + 14: two circles